M000190996

William Roulston began working for the Ulster Historical Foundation in 1997 and has been Research Director since 2006. He was awarded a PhD in Archaeology by Queen's University Belfast in 2004. He has written and edited a number of publications on different aspects of Irish and in particular Ulster history. These include: *Foyle Valley Covenanters* (2015), *Researching Scots-Irish Ancestors* (2nd edition, 2018), (co-author) *Exiles of '98: Ulster Presbyterians and the United States* (2018), *'The Insolence of Dissenters?' Religious Controversy in Ballintoy in 1716* (2018), and (co-editor) *Transatlantic Lives: The Irish Experience in Colonial America* (2019). He is a Member of Council of the Presbyterian Historical Society of Ireland and is the Convener of the Reformed Presbyterian Church History Committee. Raised on a farm in Bready, County Tyrone, he now lives with his family near Cullybackey, County Antrim.

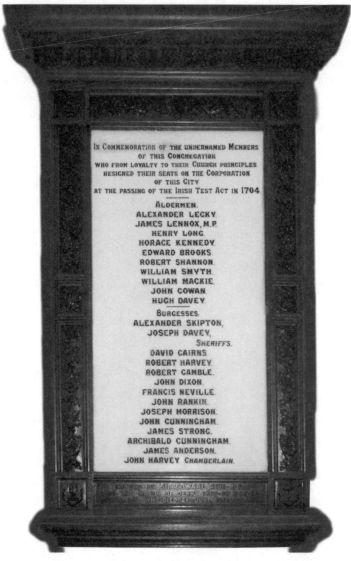

Memorial in the vestibule of First Derry Presbyterian Church
(Courtesy of Mark Thompson)

Researching
Presbyterian Ancestors
in Ireland

William J. Roulston

ULSTER HISTORICAL FOUNDATION

FRONT COVER
Bready Reformed Presbyterian Church, County Tyrone, late 1800s
(from Samuel Ferguson, *Brief Biographical Sketches of Some Covenanting
Ministers Who Laboured During the Latter Half of the Eighteenth Century* (1898))

BACK COVER
Page from a Psalm tune book created by Elizabeth Stevenson
of Gortmellan, County Tyrone, 1799

Plaque on Gortin Presbyterian Church, County Tyrone

Title of a list of members and adherents of the Reformed Presbyterian
Church in Derry, 1848 (PRONI, CR5/13/8/1)

INSIDE FRONT COVER
1642 Presbytery Memorial, Carrickfergus, County Antrim
Page from the Session book of the Antrim (Covenanter) Congregation

Published 2020
by Ulster Historical Foundation
www.ancestryireland.com
www.booksireland.org.uk

Except as otherwise permitted under the Copyright, Designs and Patents Act
1988, this publication may only be reproduced, stored or transmitted in any
form or by any means with the prior permission in writing of the publisher or,
in the case of reprographic reproduction, in accordance with the terms of a
licence issued by The Copyright Licensing Agency. Enquiries concerning
reproduction outside those terms should be sent to the publisher.

© William J. Roulston and Ulster Historical Foundation
ISBN 978-1-909556-85-0

DESIGN AND FORMATTING
FPM Publishing

COVER DESIGN
J. P. Morrison

PRINTED BY
Bell & Bain Limited

Contents

Preface and acknowledgements

This book was written mainly during the 'lockdown' of spring and early summer 2020. Drawing on my research notes, and having retrieved half a dozen boxes of congregational histories from the library of the Ulster Historical Foundation – many of them donated to the Foundation through the generosity of Professor Richard Clarke – I set about writing a book on Irish Presbyterians and their records. What made my task easier was the efforts of so many people to preserve and catalogue records and, through the written word, tell the story of Presbyterians on this island. Despite the loss of many records through neglect and carelessness and, in a few cases, downright villainy, a vast treasure trove of material is available for the researcher.

In the opening years of the twentieth century the far-sightedness of a number of individuals led to the formation of the Presbyterian Historical Society of Ireland. In more than two decades of using the Society's library and archive I have been assisted by a succession of dedicated and capable librarians. The current incumbent, Valerie Adams, has brought a wealth of experience to the role and has steered the Society into the digital age. Likewise the Public Record Office of Northern Ireland deserves enormous credit for accessioning Presbyterian records from its opening in the 1920s and, beginning in the early 1960s, for undertaking a massive programme of microfilming Presbyterian baptism and marriage registers and other congregational documents. I wish to acknowledge the tremendous assistance given to me by the staff of PRONI over the last quarter of a century.

References to original documents are contained within the main text, and unless otherwise stated are for items held at PRONI. It should be noted that in some archives much material is held off-site and needs to be ordered in advance. Occasionally documents go missing – which usually means misplaced – and at times records are closed on preservation grounds. If wishing to clarify if a particular document is available for inspection, it is best to contact the relevant archive in advance of a visit. Researchers should also be aware that until 1752 the new year in Ireland did not begin until 25 March and should take this into consideration when looking at sources prior to this date. References to publications are contained in the endnotes to each chapter. For the most part these are in an abbreviated format, especially when citing from a congregational history when the details provided comprise name of author, name of congregation and the relevant page number(s). The full details of the book will be found in the Bibliography.

Over the years many people have drawn my attention to records relating to Irish Presbyterianism and have helped me to understand something of their significance. First of all, I owe an enormous debt to Dr Brian Trainor whose enthusiasm for making archives accessible to all was second to none. I continue to be grateful to my colleagues at the Ulster Historical Foundation for their interest and encouragement. At the risk of overlooking someone (for which I apologise sincerely), I would also like to thank the following: Geoffrey Allen, Linda Ballard, Raymond Blair, Godfrey Brown, the late Bill Crawford, Tim Donachie, the late Eull Dunlop, Brian Dunwoody, John Erskine, Peter Gilmore, Tom Gribben, Robert Heslip, Jack Johnston, John Lockington, Linde Lunney, Alison McCaughan, Trevor McCavery, Robert McCollum, Leslie McKeague, Richard MacMaster, Trevor Magee, Brian Mitchell, James Moffett, Ian Montgomery, John Nelson, John O'Neill, Donald Patton, Ivor Smith, Brendan Scott and Mark Thompson. Finally, my greatest debt is to my own family – to my wife Heather, son Harry and daughter Sarah for putting up with my historical excursions, and to my parents to whom this book is dedicated.

Abbreviations

Note on nomenclature

Throughout this book the word Presbyterian has been used in a general sense to refer to the members of religious denominations in Ireland following the presbyterian form of church government. On account of their rejection of the episcopalian Established Church (Church of Ireland) they were commonly known as Dissenters and non-conformists, especially in the eighteenth century. In addition, the adherents of particular churches have acquired various epithets. For example, Reformed Presbyterians are known as Covenanters, while Non-Subscribing Presbyterians have often been called Unitarians.

1

Introduction:

The many shades of Irish Presbyterianism

Presbyterians have been living in Ireland for over four centuries and have made an immense contribution to the history of this island. For many people there is an understandable confusion at the bewildering array of manifestations of Presbyterianism in Ireland – Seceder, Non-Subscribing, Reformed, Free, and Evangelical. The aim of this Introduction, therefore, is to provide a brief overview of the historic Presbyterian denominations, focusing on their origins and important developments in their structures and governance. More detailed studies of the Presbyterian churches in Ireland are highlighted in the Bibliography of this book.

1.1 The Presbyterian Church in Ireland

In 1536 Henry VIII was declared 'the only supreme head in earth of the whole church in Ireland,' marking the formal beginning of the Reformation in Ireland. To begin with Protestantism made little progress in Ireland and on the whole it failed to win the hearts and minds of the Irish population, most of whom remained adherents of Catholicism. In 1566 the English administration based in Dublin invited the most high profile figure in the Scottish Reformation, John Knox, to Ireland to conduct a preaching tour. Knox was open to the idea, but in the end he was unable to undertake the journey.[1] By the late sixteenth century the first Presbyterians in Ireland can be identified, among them the Englishman Walter Travers, who was appointed the provost of Trinity College Dublin in 1594.[2] However, the established or state church – the Church of Ireland – was organised along episcopalian rather than presbyterian lines.

In the early seventeenth century, with the influx of large numbers of Scottish settlers, a number of ministers with presbyterian convictions arrived in Ulster from Scotland. Settling at Ballycarry in east Antrim in 1613, Edward Brice[3] is counted the first and others who followed included Robert Cunningham at Holywood, Robert Blair at Bangor and John Livingston at Killinchy. To begin with these men were accommodated within the Church of Ireland and were allowed a certain amount of freedom to organise their congregations along presbyterian lines. However, in the 1630s there were moves to bring the Church of Ireland more closely into line with the Church of England and those clergymen who held to presbyterian beliefs were expelled for refusing to accept this. In Scotland attempts by Charles I to impose his authority upon the Church provoked a hostile response which eventually led to the National Covenant of 1638, which received much support from the Scottish community in Ulster.

In 1642 an army from Scotland landed at Carrickfergus to defend Scottish settlers from attacks from the Irish in the wake of the uprising that began in October of the previous year. Accompanying this army were several Presbyterian ministers acting as chaplains, and in June 1642 these ministers, along with a number of elders, established the inaugural Irish Presbytery, from which, in a formal sense, today's Presbyterian churches in Ireland descend. In 1644 the Solemn League and Covenant, which had been prepared in 1643 by Scottish Covenanters and English Parliamentarians, was brought to Ireland where it was subscribed to by many thousands of people, especially in areas where Scottish settlement was heaviest.[4] From the mid-1650s, during the period known as the Commonwealth, there was greater freedom of worship and many ministers in Ulster were Scottish Presbyterians. The original Ulster Presbytery was divided into a series of regional 'meetings' and in 1659 representatives of these gathered in Ballymena for what was in essence the first meeting of a Presbyterian synod in Ulster.[5]

Following the Restoration of 1660, ministers who refused to conform to the teachings and episcoplian government of the newly reinstated Church of Ireland were dismissed. Despite periods of persecution, Presbyterians continued to form congregations and from around 1670 they began to build their own places of worship. Nonetheless, after 1661 there were no further meetings of a

Presbyterian synod until 1690; the earliest records of the Synod of Ulster date from 1691. The 1690s witnessed a major influx of Scots into Ireland, encouraged in part by harvest crises in their native land. By the end of the seventeenth century, therefore, Presbyterians were numerically superior to Anglicans across much of Ulster, and this was a major source of concern for both the government and the Established Church.[6]

Though the Penal Laws passed by the Irish Parliament did not impact on them as harshly as on Catholics, Presbyterians felt aggrieved at legislation which restricted their rights and freedoms in certain areas. Presbyterians were particularly angered when the provisions of the Test Act were extended to Ireland in 1704. Henceforth those wishing to hold civil and military office had to produce evidence that they had taken communion in the Church of Ireland; this effectively disbarred Presbyterians from such positions. Presbyterians also resented having to pay the tithes that were demanded by the Church of Ireland clergy. Even after the passing of the Toleration Act in 1719, which allowed Presbyterians to attend their own places of worship without being penalised, there was a strong sense of estrangement from the Anglican and landed establishment, and this was a contributory factor in the large-scale emigration of Presbyterians from Ulster to America in the early eighteenth century. In time, however, these laws were repealed, though it was not until 1843 that all marriages conducted by Presbyterian ministers were given full legal recognition.

While much of the historical focus on Presbyterians in Ireland has been on the northern province of Ulster, Presbyterians were to be found in the rest of the island, though in smaller numbers and mainly in cities and towns. There, for historical reasons, the influences of English rather than Scottish traditions were stronger and there were differences in doctrine and in religious practice.[7] In 1696 the Presbytery of Munster was formed by congregations in the provinces of Leinster and Munster. Ministers in Dublin joined this body to form the Southern Association. The relationship between northern and southern Presbyterians is one that is not easy to define. For instance, at least in the early years of the eighteenth century, it was possible for a Dublin minister to be both a member of the Southern Association and the Synod of Ulster. In his survey of Presbyterianism in Ireland of

1803, Rev. William Campbell penned the following observations on northern and southern Presbyterians: 'These churches have always remained distinct, as they were distinct in their origin; but still maintained an occasional intercourse, and always a friendly correspondence.'[8]

In the early nineteenth century, the relationship between theological conservatives and liberals within the Synod of Ulster became increasingly fraught and culminated in the withdrawal of 17 liberal ministers and their congregations in 1829 (see below). Their departure and the increasing emphasis on doctrinal orthodoxy in the Synod of Ulster were among the factors that paved the way for the union of this Synod with the Secession Synod (see below). On 10 July 1840 these bodies united to form the General Assembly of the Presbyterian Church in Ireland, totalling over 430 congregations and some 650,000 members. Today the Presbyterian Church is the second largest Protestant denomination in Ireland with more than 530 congregations, overwhelmingly in Northern Ireland (where it is the largest Protestant denomination), but also in other parts of the island, especially counties Donegal and Monaghan as well as the city and environs of Dublin.

1.2 The Non-Subscribing Presbyterian Church

The origins of the Non-Subscribing Presbyterian Church can be traced to a dispute within the Synod of Ulster over the issue of subscription to the Westminster Confession of Faith, the statement of doctrine of the Presbyterian Church. Led by the Rev. John Abernethy of Antrim, those who denied the necessity of subscribing to this work were known as 'New Light' Presbyterians or 'non-subscribers'. Failing to reach a consensus on the issue, in 1725 the Synod of Ulster placed the non-subscribing ministers in the Presbytery of Antrim (this did not mean that all of them were in County Antrim). In the following year the Synod decided that it could no longer 'maintain ministerial communion' with the Presbytery of Antrim. However, there continued to be a rather nebulous relationship between the two bodies.

The subscription controversy created rancour and division in some congregations. In Belfast the ministers of both the First and Second congregations were non-subscribers, which led to the formation of the Third Congregation in the early 1720s. Some congregations that had been placed in the Presbytery of Antrim reverted to the Synod of Ulster. The issue of subscription was not limited to northern congregations. In 1726 the subscribing ministers in Dublin were formed into the Presbytery of Dublin within the Synod of Ulster. Non-subscribing ministers in Dublin established (or revived?) the Southern Presbytery of Dublin in 1773. In 1809 the Synod of Munster, a non-subscribing body, was formed by the Presbytery of Munster and the Southern Presbytery of Dublin.[9]

A century after the formation of the Presbytery of Antrim the issue of subscription, bound up with Arianism with its denial of the divinity of Christ, again arose within the Synod of Ulster. The leading figures on each side of the debate were Rev. Henry Cooke for the orthodox party, and Rev. Henry Montgomery for the liberals. The decisive debate took place in August 1829 and resulted in victory for Cooke as the great majority of the members of the Synod of Ulster backed him. This led to the withdrawal of Montgomery and 16 other ministers and their congregations from the Synod of Ulster and the creation of the Remonstrant Synod of Ulster in 1830.[10] As was the case a hundred years earlier, the disagreements led to splits in a number of congregations and protracted legal disputes over the possession of meeting houses. In 1835 the Remonstrant Synod, the Presbytery of Antrim and the Synod of Munster came together to form the Association of Irish Non-Subscribing Presbyterians. Though remaining separate entities, these bodies worked together on a range of initiatives and experienced numerical growth as new congregations were founded. However, divisions between non-subscribers over issues such as the limits of their theological liberty resulted in the creation of new bodies.

In the early 1860s several congregations withdrew from the Remonstrant Synod and were received into the Presbytery of Antrim. However, this only led to the departure of a number of congregations in the Presbytery of Antrim to form the more conservative Northern Presbytery of Antrim in 1862. A further separation occurred in 1871 when five congregations left the Presbytery of Antrim over the form of church government and established the Free Congregational Union. Despite these divisions, in the early 1900s there were moves to unite the different bodies of non-subscribers. Eventually, in February 1910, the formal inauguration of the General Synod of the Non-Subscribing Presbyterian Church took place in First Presbyterian

Church, Belfast. In 1935 this body was joined by the Synod of Munster. Today there are over 30 congregations in the Non-Subscribing Presbyterian Church, divided between the Presbytery of Antrim, Presbytery of Bangor and Synod of Munster.

1.3 The Secession Church

The largest of the three smaller historic branches of Presbyterianism in Ireland was the Secession Church. Its origins can be traced to a dispute in the Church of Scotland over the issue of patronage. In 1733 a number of ministers of the Church of Scotland seceded (hence their appellation Seceders) in 1733 and formed the Associate Presbytery. The conservative evangelicalism of the Seceders appealed to many Presbyterians in Ulster and from the 1740s onwards Seceder congregations were established here. As a general rule, it would appear that it was in those areas most strongly affected by the influx of families from Scotland in the years either side of 1700 that the Seceders made the greatest impact.

The first Seceder congregation in Ireland was at Lylehill, County Antrim. In 1741, Presbyterians in this district appealed to the Associate Presbytery in Scotland to send them preachers. Occasional preaching supplies were provided for several years before Isaac Patton, a native of Myroe, near Limavady, was ordained their minister in 1746. The Seceders in Scotland divided over the issue of the Burgess Oath, giving rise to the Burghers and Antiburghers. Though this division had little relevance to Ireland, nonetheless, the Seceders here separated into the two camps. The Irish Burghers established a Synod at a meeting in Monaghan in 1779 and the Antiburghers did so in Belfast in 1788. These Secession bodies united in 1818 and, as noted above, in 1840 the Secession Synod joined with the Synod of Ulster in forming the General Assembly.

The Seceders were especially prone to divisions, both in Scotland and Ireland, giving rise to new Secession denominations. A few of the more important of these in Ireland are considered briefly below.

The Associate Presbytery/United Presbyterian Church

The decision of the Seceders to accept the *Regium Donum* (a bounty paid to Presbyterian ministers) on the basis of the classification set out by the government proved controversial. Opposition was led by Rev.

James Bryce of Killaig and resulted in the formation of the Associate Presbytery *c.* 1810, which consisted of a small number of congregations mainly in counties Antrim and Londonderry. In 1858 a union was formed with United Presbyterian Church in Scotland (itself the product of a merger in 1847 of the Relief Church and the United Secession Synod) and the Associate Presbytery became the United Presbyterian Presbytery of Ireland. In 1900 the United Presbyterian Church joined with the Free Church of Scotland to create the United Free Church. By the early 1920s there was a feeling that the United Free Church congregations in Ireland should unite with the General Assembly of the Presbyterian Church as there was little to separate them. In 1922 the United Free Church Presbytery of Ireland agreed formally to adopt this position. While there was reticence on the part of some of the Irish congregations to break the link with Scotland, in the end most of them joined the General Assembly (though the congregation in Cullybackey joined the Methodist Church).

Original Secession Synod[11]

The decision of the Secession Synod to form a union with the Synod of Ulster in 1840 was not unanimous. Initially 16 Secession ministers opposed the move on various grounds, though half these men joined the General Assembly in the following year and another did so in 1845. Though they came to be known as the Original Seceders, those who remained outside of the General Assembly did not believe that they had established a new denomination – rather they were continuing the Irish Secession Church. The congregations of Original Secession Synod were divided into two presbyteries – Markethill and Monaghan – a reflection of the fact that they were concentrated principally in south Ulster, though in actual fact these presbyteries usually held joint meetings. Originally there were seven congregations, though at one point in the mid 1870s there were a dozen. The last congregation to be founded was Belfast in 1875. In the early twentieth century most of the Original Secession congregations joined the General Assembly, though two joined the Reformed Presbyterian Church. By 1926 only one congregation remained – Coronary in County Cavan – and it was taken under the care of the Presbytery of Ayr in Scotland. However, in 1955 Coronary was received into the General Assembly.

United Original Secession Synod

One final Secession body that may be mentioned here was the United Original Secession Synod, to which a small number of congregations in Ireland belonged. These congregations had been formed in the early 1800s and owed their origins to disputes over the *Regium Donum* and other issues. In 1842 a Presbytery of Down and Derry was established. However, in 1851 one of the congregations, Boardmills, joined the General Assembly, while in 1852 two others, Ballylintagh and Garvagh, joined the Free Church of Scotland, where they spent 11 years before they too joined the General Assembly. That left Toberdoney and Dromore (County Londonderry), the latter formed by those who disagreed with the decision of Ballylintagh to join the Free Church of Scotland. These two congregations remained with the United Original Secession Synod until that body joined the Church of Scotland in 1956, whereupon they were admitted to the General Assembly of the Presbyterian Church in Ireland.

1.4 The Reformed Presbyterian (Covenanter) Church

The Covenanter or Reformed Presbyterian Church was composed of those who adhered most strongly to the aforementioned Covenants of 1638 and 1643. Of critical importance for Reformed Presbyterians was the belief in the descending obligation of the Covenants from one generation to the next (a belief not shared by the majority of Presbyterians). Thus while the Revolution Settlement of 1689–90 established the Church of Scotland along presbyterian lines, its failure to recognise the continuing validity of the Covenants resulted in a minority rejecting the political and religious establishments. In Ireland too, especially in the province of Ulster, there were groups of Covenanters. In the 1670s and 1680s, during a period of intense persecution in Scotland, many individuals and families found refuge in the north of Ireland, strengthening numerically the position of the Covenanters on the island.

Information on the Covenanters in Ireland prior to the second half of the eighteenth century is limited in the extreme. There were no ordained ministers, no organised congregations, and no meeting houses. There are a few references to Ireland in the records of the Scottish Covenanters, though these are of a fairly general nature. The survival of Irish Covenanter identity during this period was due in no small measure to the adoption of the 'society' system. A Covenanter 'society' was composed of a group of families living in the same geographical area. The strength of this system was such that for over 60 years, in the absence of resident ministers and meeting houses, Covenanters in Ireland were able to maintain a separate existence. Meetings were held in homes, with larger assemblies held in the open-air. The 'society' system continued into the nineteenth century and many Reformed Presbyterian records of this era are organised by 'society'.

It was not until 1757 that the first Reformed Presbyterian minister, Rev. William Martin, was ordained in Ireland. To begin with Martin ministered to Covenanter societies scattered from County Donegal to County Down. However, in 1760 the Covenanters in Ireland were divided into two congregations. Martin chose the 'Antrim Congregation' and based himself at Kellswater, near Ballymena, where a former mill was renovated as a meeting house. In 1763 a second Covenanter minister was ordained and the first Reformed Presbytery was established in Ireland. This presbytery was dissolved in 1779 following the emigration to America of several of its ministers and the deaths of others. However, in 1792 the Irish Reformed Presbytery was reconstituted. In 1810 it was agreed to divide the Reformed Presbyterian Church of Ireland into four presbyteries (Northern, Southern, Eastern and Western), and to form a synod which would have oversight of these presbyteries (this structure continues to this day). In May 1811 12 ministers and nine elders, representing nearly 30 congregations and preaching stations, gathered in Cullybackey for the inaugural Synod of the Reformed Presbyterian Church of Ireland. Today there are around 40 Reformed Presbyterian congregations in Ireland, exclusively in Ulster apart from one in Galway.

Eastern Reformed Presbyterian Church

In 1840 there was a split in the Reformed Presbyterian Church over the accepted Covenanter view of the powers and responsibilities of the civil magistrate (i.e. the government) in spiritual matters as set forth in the Westminster Confession of Faith and the Catechisms. Several ministers and their congregations withdrew from the Reformed Presbyterian Synod and, in October 1842, formed the Eastern Reformed Presbyterian Synod. The Eastern Synod comprised two presbyteries – Belfast and Derry – and at its height numbered about ten congregations. The Eastern Reformed Presbyterian Church began to disintegrate in the late nineteenth century and its demise was complete by the end of the first decade of the twentieth. Some congregations simply faded away. The rest either joined the General Assembly of the Presbyterian Church or returned to the Reformed Presbyterian Church.[12]

1.5 Other Presbyterian denominations

A number of other Presbyterian denominations have established a witness in Ireland. For over a century there was a congregation of the Presbyterian Church of Wales in Dublin. Having used the Lutheran church in Dublin for a number of years, as well as some other venues, a place of worship for the congregation was erected in Talbot Street in 1838. The congregation closed in the summer of 1939.[13] Two further Presbyterian denominations in Ireland were founded in the twentieth century. In 1927 Rev. J. Ernest Davey, a professor at the Presbyterian College in Belfast, was accused of espousing doctrines that ran contrary to the traditional teachings of the Church. Though acquitted of heresy, a minority dissented from this verdict and withdrew to form the Irish Evangelical Church (since 1964 the Evangelical Presbyterian Church), of which there are nine congregations today. In 1951 Rev. Ian Paisley founded the Free Presbyterian Church of Ulster, which numbers over 60 congregations in Ireland.

Notes

[1] Jane Dawson, *John Knox* (2015), pp 258–9.

[2] Linde Lunney, 'The history of Dublin Presbyterianism', *Familia: Ulster Genealogical Review*, vol. 34 (2018), p. 131.

[3] J. W. Nelson, *Edward Brice and the Origins of Presbyterianism in Ireland* (2013).

[4] The copy of the Covenant signed at Holywood in 1644 is in the collection of the Ulster Museum in Belfast.

[5] According to an early historian of Presbyterianism in Ireland, Rev. Patrick Adair, 'Some called it the General Presbetry, some called it a Synod': Robert Armstrong *et al.*, *Presbyterian History in Ireland: Two Seventeenth-Century Narratives* (2016), p. 222.

6 For more on this period, see Raymond Gillespie, 'The Presbyterian Revolution in Ulster, 1600–1690', in W. J. Shiels and Diana Wood (eds), *The Churches, Ireland and the Irish: Studies in Church History XXV* (1989), pp 159–70.

7 English Presbyterians in Ireland are considered in Phil Kilroy, *Protestant Dissent and Controversy in Ireland, 1660–1714* (1994), pp 35–59.

8 William Campbell, *Sketches of the History of Presbyterianism in Ireland* (2019), p. 172.

9 A subsequent Presbytery of Munster was formed in 1840 by ministers who withdrew from the Synod of Munster; in 1854 this body joined the General Assembly.

10 J. W. Nelson, 'The parting of the ways', *BPHSI*, vol. 34 (2010).

11 Godfrey Brown, *The Last of the Seceders: The Original Secession Church in Ireland, 1841–1956* (2017).

12 William Roulston, *Forgotten Covenanters: The Rise and Fall of the Eastern Reformed Presbyterian Church* (forthcoming).

13 See the chapter on the Presbyterian Church of Wales in Steven Smyrl's *Dictionary of Dublin Dissent* (2009).

2

Presbyterian congregations

When I heard that the Synod of Ulster wished for a particular account of their congregations, I thought I could give some useful hints relative to Templepatrick. When I attended particularly to the subject, I found that more attention and research were necessary than I first supposed ...

S. M. Stephenson, 1825[1]

The basic organisational unit within the various strands of Presbyterianism in Ireland is the congregation. Each congregation is composed of families and individuals living in the same geographical area, ranging from those in full communicant membership to people whose connection might only be nominal. The place of worship for the congregation is usually a separate building known traditionally as a meeting house. The body with spiritual oversight of the congregation is the Session, composed of the minister and ruling elders. Other congregational bodies include committees established to oversee various activities, Sunday schools, and social and recreational groups. In the presbyterian system congregations are grouped together to form presbyteries.

2.1 The formation of congregations

As Chapter 1 has shown, the oldest Presbyterian congregations in Ireland can be traced back to the seventeenth century. By 1690 around 90 congregations had been established on the island, the great majority of which were in Ulster and especially in areas where the settlement of families from Scotland had made the greatest impact. Since then hundreds more congregations have been established. To a large extent the founding of new congregations was a response to the rise in the Presbyterian population in many parts of the island through natural increase over time and the movement of Presbyterian families into new areas. For example, in the late seventeenth and early eighteenth centuries many adherents of Presbyterianism settled in County Monaghan, leading to the formation of congregations at such places as Ballybay, Carrickmaclim and Stonebridge.

The formation of a new congregation was a major decision at many levels and the impact of this step on existing congregations was taken into consideration. Prior to the formation of new congregation at Armoy around 1770 the minister of nearby Kilraughts was asked if it 'would be hurtful to neighbouring congregations'; he answered that it would not.[2] Not all congregations were so accommodating and there were frequent protests from existing congregations about the formation of new ones. The practicality of travelling to a convenient meeting house was also used as an argument in support of the formation of a new congregation. In 1717 the need for a congregation in Seapatrick (Banbridge) was due to 'it not being practicable for them to go elsewhere in winter, because of great waters.'[3]

Some were founded as a result of divisions within the main body of Presbyterians. When the non-subscribers in the Synod of Ulster were placed in the Presbytery of Antrim in 1725 a number of congregations divided. For instance, 90 families withdrew from the congregation of Antrim, the minister of which was the non-subscriber Rev. John Abernethy, and formed a new congregation in 1726 (today's First Antrim). A century later another subscription controversy, which led to the formation of the Remonstrant Synod, also resulted in congregational splits in such places as Cairncastle, Clough (County Down) and Killinchy. Disputes within congregations over a variety of issues could result in permanent or at least long-term divisions. The congregation of Donagheady split in 1741 due to a disagreement over the choice of a new minister. Absurdly the meeting houses of First Donagheady and Second Donagheady were only a few hundred yards apart; the congregations reunited in 1933.

With the emergence of new Presbyterian denominations, those of the Seceders and the Covenanters (Reformed Presbyterians), new congregations were established. The first Seceder congregation in Ireland was formed in the 1740s and dozens more were founded in the following decades. When the two main branches of Seceders united in 1818 there were nearly 100 congregations in the Secession Synod. In 1800 there were more than 20 Reformed Presbyterian congregations in Ireland, there having been none half a century earlier. The first half of the nineteenth century was a period of major expansion for the Presbyterian churches in Ireland with formation of many new congregations. Some of what was driving this growth was the mission work within Ireland, especially in the south and west of the island. In these regions the number of congregations rose from 17 in 1841 to 39 two decades later.[4]

The growth of towns and cities also resulted in the founding of new congregations. This is especially apparent in Belfast. In 1800, when the population was around 20,000, there were only five congregations of the different branches of Presbyterianism in Belfast. However, in 1900, when the city's population was about 350,000, there were more than 50 congregations of the General Assembly alone, and a further 11 churches of the smaller Presbyterian denominations.[5] The population of the city of Derry was considerably smaller than that of Belfast, totalling just under 40,000 in 1901 when there were nine Presbyterian congregations, an increase from two a century earlier. Depending on where one draws the limits of Dublin, the number of congregations in that city at the beginning of the twentieth century was around a dozen, with slightly over half having been founded in the 1800s.

While many congregations can look back on over 300 years of witness, some Presbyterian congregations had a comparatively brief existence and have left either no records at all, or else very few. In 1791, as the result of a falling out between Rev. George McEwen and some of his flock, a section of the congregation of Killinchy withdrew and built a meeting house at Lisbane. The 'New Erection', as it was known, lasted only a few years. It was never recognised officially by the Synod of Ulster and following the death of McEwen in 1795 the dissidents returned to Killinchy; the meeting house at Lisbane was later used as a barn.[6] In the 1840s there was an attempt to establish a congregation in Killowen, Coleraine. A site for a meeting house was secured from the landlord, the Clothworkers' Company of London, and in 1842 building work began. In the same year Rev. John Turbitt, was installed as pastor. However, the construction work stalled and Turbitt resigned and emigrated to America. A second minister, Rev. Arthur Fullerton was installed in 1846. However, when the

Clothworkers' Company learned that so little progress had been made with the meeting house they took back possession of the site and refused any further assistance. Fullerton resigned in 1849, effectively bringing an end to the congregation.[7]

2.2 The boundaries of congregations

Though in the early days of organised Presbyterianism in Ireland there was some attempt to use the existing network of parishes as the geographical basis of a congregation, this proved impracticable to maintain. For one thing, not every parish, even those of considerable extent, had a Presbyterian congregation. For instance, there was no Presbyterian congregation in the parish of Leckpatrick, County Tyrone, prior to the nineteenth century, but there was a congregation in the parish to the north, Donagheady, and another in the parish to the south, Camus-juxta-Mourne (Strabane). In 1729, it was settled that the boundary between the congregations of Donagheady and Strabane should be the burn, now known as the Glenmornan River, which flowed, roughly speaking, through the centre of Leckpatrick parish. See Chapter 6.2 for the detailed way in which the bounds of the new congregation of Coagh were defined by the Synod of Ulster in 1709.

At different times the minutes of the meetings of presbyteries and the Synod of Ulster include references to the Presbyterian families in particular townlands being transferred from one congregation to another. The reasons included attempts to strengthen weaker congregations, though inevitably some people were left dissatisfied at the decisions made. The way in which a new congregation drew families from existing churches is demonstrated clearly in the case of Claggan, which was established in 1846. The original membership of Claggan comprised 23 members from First Cookstown, four from Second Cookstown, 21 from Third Cookstown, four from First Moneymore, three from Second Moneymore, and four from Orritor.[8]

The defining of boundaries for congregations in the General Assembly continued into the twentieth century. For instance, in 1917 the boundaries of the congregation of Killeter Presbyterian Church were specified as:

From Mournebeg Bridge by straight line to Killen Corner; by road to Ednasop Corner, Carrickmedew, Lough Lack to Rushinbane Corner;

by straight line to Civil Parish Boundary at top of Lough Derg; by Civil Parish Boundary to Kelly's Bridge; by straight line to Barnesmore Station; by railway to Croaghonagh Cross Roads; by straight line to Civil Parish Boundary at Pullan's Mountain; by straight line to Mournebeg Bridge.[9]

From the above description it will be seen that topographical and man-made features, combined with administrative divisions, were used to define the boundaries of the congregation.

2.3 The names of congregations

The name of a congregation usually derives from the locality in which it is found. Many of the oldest congregations bear parish names, indicative, at least in part, of the fact that they were founded at a time when the organisation of the church was much more closely linked to the parish system. Others may have borne a parish name originally, but this was changed subsequently. For example, Monreagh was originally Taughboyne, the name of the parish in this part of Donegal. Other congregations take their name from the town or village, or the townland or district in which they are found. Two Reformed Presbyterian congregations are named after the river that flows by the meeting house – Faughan and Kellswater. A few congregations have names that can only be explained with some local knowledge. In 1838 the congregation of Albany was formed. The name seems to have been chosen in deference to Lord Castlestewart, the major landowner in the area and a supporter of the work, whose ancestors were the Dukes of Albany.[10]

A few congregations have changed names over the years. For instance, around 1700 a congregation was founded in south County Monaghan and a meeting house was built at Carrickmaclim. In the late 1830s the decision was made to abandon this meeting house and build a new place of worship at Corvally, which would be more convenient for the majority of the families in the congregation. This meeting house was completed in 1839 and continues in use to the present day. Eventually, in 1880, the name of the congregation was changed to Corvally. Founded in 1727, New Row Presbyterian Church in Coleraine takes its name from a row of tenements built in the early seventeenth century. Though popularly known as New Row for many years, it was only in 1959 that the congregation's name was changed officially to this; originally it was called simply the 'New Erection' and later Second Coleraine.[11]

Researchers are often baffled by the different designations (i.e. First, Second, Old, etc) given to many congregations. If a town or district had both a Synod of Ulster congregation and a Seceder congregation, typically the former became known as the First Presbyterian Church and the latter the Second Presbyterian Church following the Union of the Synods in 1840. There are, of course, exceptions to this rule. Furthermore, some congregations changed designation. For instance, when a new Synod of Ulster congregation was founded in Rathfriland in 1833 it was called Second Rathfriland. However, following the Union of the Synods, Second Rathfriland became Third, and the Secession congregation became Second.[12]

In a number of instances, and for historical reasons, a Non-Subscribing Presbyterian Church will be known as the First or Old Presbyterian Church. The Non-Subscribing congregation in Rosemary Street, Belfast, for example, is generally known as the First Presbyterian Church, while that in Ballycarry is called the Old Presbyterian Church. However, not every congregation designated Old is a Non-Subscribing Church. For example, there is a General Assembly church in Randalstown named the Old Congregation. More than 20 Presbyterian churches across Ireland have been referred to as the 'Scots Church' (or Scottish Church, Scotch Church, etc). The reasons for the use of this term include a desire to emphasise doctrinal orthodoxy, the involvement of Scots in the foundation of the congregation, or simply because of Presbyterianism's historic links with Scotland.

2.4 *A History of Congregations*

An indispensable guide for those researching Irish Presbyterianism is *A History of Congregations in the Presbyterian Church in Ireland, 1610–1982*, published by the Presbyterian Historical Society in 1982.[13] It provides brief sketches of each of the congregations of the General Assembly of the Presbyterian Church in Ireland. It therefore includes the following congregations: those that were part of the Synod of Ulster at the founding of the General Assembly in 1840; Secession congregations that joined the General Assembly at its formation or in the years that followed; and congregations established since the General Assembly came into being. A *Supplement of Additions, Emendations and Corrections with an Index* was published in association with the Ulster Historical Foundation in 1996. This includes a few congregations that were overlooked in the original publication. The text of both publications has been combined and can now be accessed by members of the Presbyterian Historical Society via the PHSI website.

The primary foci of the brief histories contained in the *History of Congregations* are on the origins of the church and the succession of ministers, though other developments may also be included, such as the construction of a new meeting house. Other than those of the ministers, comparatively few names of individuals are included. Since there are two or more Presbyterian congregations in many larger towns and villages, especially in the north of Ireland, the *History of Congregations* is particularly useful in working out their chronology and how they relate to one another. Newtownards, for example, has several Presbyterian congregations. First Newtownards is the oldest and dates back to the seventeenth century. Second Newtownards originally had Seceder connections, while Regent Street was established in 1834. The formation of the Greenwell Street congregation can be linked to the 1859 Revival. Strean Presbyterian Church outside the town came into existence following a disagreement in First Newtownards in 1865. It was named after its main instigator, Thomas Strean, who gave over £8,000 to build a meeting house.

There is no equivalent volume for the Non-Subscribing Presbyterian Church. However, for the Reformed Presbyterian Church there is *The Covenanters in Ireland: A History of the Congregations* (2010). The congregational histories are arranged by presbytery – Northern, Southern, Eastern and Western – and each of them includes details on the origin of the congregation, the succession of ministers, the place of worship (including photographs), and the names of elders. The book also includes Reformed Presbyterian churches no longer in existence. Shorter sections cover the Presbytery of New Brunswick and Nova Scotia, the Presbytery of Australia, the Reformed Presbyterian Church in England, the Irish Mission, the Foreign Mission and the Reformed Presbyterian Church in France.

2.5 Congregational histories

In his book, *The Shaping of Ulster Presbyterian Belief and Practice*, the historian Dr Andrew Holmes has observed that there is a 'seemingly unique obsession of Ulster Presbyterians with writing and reading congregational histories' (p. 27). To a large extent this is a reflection of the importance of the congregation within the Presbyterian system, and the way in which its identity is intertwined with its locality and the families who, often for generations, have been associated with it. The best collection of congregational histories is in the Library & Archive of the Presbyterian Historical Society of Ireland. There are also good collections of these histories at the Ulster Historical Foundation in Newtownards, the Linen Hall Library and Public Record Office of Northern Ireland in Belfast, the library of the North of Ireland Family History Society in Newtownabbey, and in the public library system managed by Libraries NI.

A wish to preserve the history of a congregation by putting its story in writing can be traced back over two centuries. At the meeting of the Synod of Ulster in 1819 the following overture was made:

That with a view to preserve a knowledge of important facts relative to the Presbyterians of Ireland, the Ministers of the Synod shall prepare accounts of their Congregations, and submit them to their respective Presbyteries. That ministers shall state the situation and extent, with the dates and circumstances of the original settlement, of their Congregations – the names of the Ministers, from the earliest period, with the dates and circumstances of their ordinations, installations, removals, depositions, and deaths — And shall particularly mention in what respects, important to Presbyterianism, any of the Ministers, or their Congregations, or any individuals belonging to their Congregations, have distinguished themselves.

They shall also give an account of Congregational records, and shall enter into such detail of facts, as they may judge proper, respecting their houses of worship, religious services, psalmody, elders, observance of Church discipline, funds, stipend paid at different periods, collections and subscriptions, zeal of their Congregations, number of families, state of education, and the numbers and influence of other denominations of Christians within their bounds.

Ministers will take notice of any other particulars respecting their Congregations, which they may consider worthy of being recorded.[14]

Though this overture was approved at the 1820 meeting of Synod – despite a counter proposal that the work be delegated to 'some individual of literary talents' – little seems to have come of it.

Some ministers and elders felt to the need to include historical details in the Session books they maintained. Rev. Isaac Adams, the first minister of Ballylinney, formed in 1834, was anxious that a record of the earliest years of the congregation should be preserved for posterity, writing in the Session book:

> For the information of those yet to come, an attempt is now made in the ninth year after its formation, to give a sketch of the origin and progress of this congregation – owing to the loss of some papers the statements may not be as full as could be desired, yet as far as can be remembered, nothing but facts shall be recorded.[15]

A short history of the Presbyterian congregation of Magherafelt was prepared in 1853 as an introduction to a new Session book (CR3/13/C/5). An account of the origins of Second Stewartstown, first written in 1871, was copied into the church minute book, having been extracted from an older and now lost set of minutes; it was later printed in a published history of Presbyterianism in Stewartstown.[16]

Histories of congregations began to appear in print in the nineteenth century. Accounts of individual churches were published regularly in the nineteenth-century periodicals of the different branches of Presbyterianism. For instance, Classon Porter, the minister of the Non-Subscribing congregation of Larne and Kilwaughter, wrote 'Congregational Memoirs' of several churches in east Antrim in the 1860s, which were published in the *Christian Unitarian*. The *Banner of Ulster*, a newspaper founded in 1842 and aimed at Presbyterians, also carried many articles on the history of individual congregations. In these ways Presbyterian history was communicated to a wide audience.

One of the earliest books to be published on the history of a Presbyterian congregation in Ireland is S. M. Stephenson's volume, *A Historical Essay on the Parish and Congregation of Templepatrick* (1825). This book does seem to have been a fruit of the 1819 overture of Synod for in his Preface the author writes, 'When I first heard that the Synod of Ulster wished for a particular account of their congregations, I thought I could give some useful hints relative to Templepatrick.'

However, when he began his investigations he realised that 'more attention and research were necessary than I first supposed.' Stephenson, who was a native of the district and had been a Presbyterian minister before giving this up for a career in medicine, drew on a range of sources in preparing his account of Templepatrick, including the original Session book dating back to 1646 (see Chapter 5 for more on this volume). Three years after producing this history Stephenson published *An Historical Essay on the Parish and Congregation of Grey-Abbey*, where he had been minister over 40 years earlier.

Since Stephenson's volumes first appeared hundreds more congregational histories have been published. They range from pamphlets to substantial volumes running to several hundred pages. One recent volume on the history of Clare Presbyterian Church extends to a mammoth 626 pages.[17] A number of writers have produced multiple histories. S. Alexander Blair authored books on First Kilraughts (two volumes), Ballymoney, Drumreagh and Garryduff in north Antrim. Rev. Prof. Adam Loughridge wrote histories of several Reformed Presbyterian congregations, including Cullybackey, Glenmanus and Kilraughts. Between them Rev. T. H. Mullin and his wife Julia produced volumes on Aghadowey, Ballyrashane, Ballywillan, Convoy, Dunluce and New Row in Coleraine, among others, in addition to which they have produced some broader histories, including studies of Coleraine (three volumes) and Limavady, which explore the Presbyterian dimension of those localities.

Obviously some histories are better than others. The best combine detailed analysis of the available church records with setting the story of the congregation in a broader historical context. A good example is Alison McCaughan's study of First Dunboe – *Heath, Hearth and Heart* (1988) – which interweaves wider social and economic developments over the past four centuries with the history of the congregation. Many histories contain a wealth of genealogical information on the families associated with the congregation, often presented through lengthy appendices. The value of these listings cannot be overstated for often information is presented that is not accessible elsewhere. For instance, Margaret E. Millar's *Presbyterianism in Buckna, 1756–1992* (1992) includes facsimile reproductions of detailed visitation records of 1849–70, which were in private possession. This book also has an appendix listing emigrants recorded in communicant rolls in the late nineteenth and early twentieth centuries, giving name, townland, destination and date.

A selection of invaluable listings of names from some other congregational histories is presented below:

S. Lyle Orr and Alex Haslett, *Historical Sketch of Ballyalbany Presbyterian Church* (1940): subscribers to a call to Rev. Thomas Clark 1751 (pp 10–12), subscribers to the fund for rebuilding the meeting house, 1787 (pp 48–50), seatholders in the church, 1804 (pp 64–9), stipend payers, 1866 (pp 83–4), subscribers to the manse fund, 1873–4 (pp 94–100), signatories to a memorial opposing the wearing of a gown by the minister, *c.* 1873 (pp 102–06)

A. G. Gordon, *Historic Memorials of the First Presbyterian Church of Belfast* (1887): includes the baptismal register, 1757–90 (pp 58–63), funeral register, 1712–36 (pp 64–94), lists of members, 1760, 1775, 1790 (pp 97–8, 101), list of subscribers to the building fund of the meeting house, 1781 (pp 99–100), list of 'The Ladys of Belfast' who subscribed for the new pulpit, 1783 (p. 100), first printed list of constituents [as members were known], 1812 (pp 102–03), constituents when Rev. J. Scott Porter began ministry, 1831 (pp 103–05), constituents when Rev. A. Gordon received a 'call', 1877 (pp 105–06), treasurers, sextons, singing-clerks, secretaries, organists (pp 122–3), subscribers to 'Central Hall', 1883 (pp 127–8)

T. H. Mullin, *The Kirk and Lands of Convoy since the Scottish Settlement* (1960): families belonging to the congregation, 1822, listed by townland (pp 177–91)

Joseph Magill and William Harold McCafferty, *Donacloney Meeting: An Historical Survey* (1950): subscribers to a meeting house fund, 1795 (pp 50–53)

Julia E. Mullin, *A History of Dunluce Presbyterian Church* (1995): persons supporting a 'call' to Rev. John Cameron, 1755 (pp 83–4)

Thomas Kilpatrick, *Millisle and Ballycopeland Presbyterian Church* (1934): list of subscriptions to the meeting house, 1773 (pp 2–7), list of seats let to members, 1776 (pp 9–13), subscribers to a 'call' to Rev. Andrew Greer, 1777 (pp 17–18), subscribers to a call to Rev. John Hanna, 1815 (pp 24–5) [all Millisle]; members of Ballycopeland, 1843 (pp 117–21)

Trevor McCavery, *A Covenant Community: A History of Newtownards Reformed Presbyterian Church* (1997): members in 1852 (p. 169),

admissions and re-admissions to membership, 1852–1997
(pp 170–80), signatories to a 'call' to Rev. S. R. Archer, 1928
(p. 186), contributors to the sustentation fund of the Eastern
Reformed Presbyterian Church [a separate RP congregation in
Newtownards], 1846–50 (pp 181–5)

Even if a congregational history does not exist in book form there may
be an article in a local history journal. For instance, T. G. F. Paterson
wrote an article on 'Presbyterianism in Armagh', which appeared in
Seanchas Ardmhacha: Journal of the Armagh Diocesan Historical Society
(vol. 19, no. 2, Golden Jubilee Issue (2003), pp 140–63). Likewise the
Journal of the County Louth Archaeological and Historical Society
includes an article by Dermot Foley on 'Presbyterianism in Drogheda,
1652–1827' (vol. 25, no. 2 (2002), pp 179–88). *The Glynns*, the
journal of the Glens of Antrim Historical Society, includes an article
by S. Alexander Blair on 'Presbyterianism in Glenarm', (vol. 9 (1981),
pp 37–51), which helpfully includes the names of some members of
the congregation in 1772. The *Bulletin of the Presbyterian Historical
Society of Ireland* also includes articles of interest on congregations, as
well as reviews of congregational histories.

A number of other studies have been published which include more
detailed information on individual congregations. Much valuable
information on congregations outside of Ulster is found in *A History
of Presbyterianism in Dublin and the South and West of Ireland* by C. H.
Irwin (1890). An earlier work is *Ordination Service ... at the
Ordination of Rev. James Martineau. With an Appendix, Containing a
Summary History of the Presbyterian Churches in the City of Dublin*
(1829). Other volumes include James McConnell, *Presbyterianism in
Belfast* (1912), which looks at congregations in the Belfast Presbytery;
Julia Mullin, *The Presbytery of Coleraine* (1979) and *The Presbytery of
Limavady* (1989); Harry C. Waddell, *The Presbytery of Route: The Ter-
Centenary Book* (1960; a revised edition was published in 2007, edited
by Godfrey Brown); Alexander Stuart Cromie, *Presbyterians in the
City of Cork* (2004); and Steven Smyrl, *Dictionary of Dublin Dissent*
(2009). Rev. A. G. Lecky's books – *The Laggan and its Presbyterianism*
(1905) and *In the Days of the Laggan Presbytery* (1908) – contain a
wealth of information on congregations in north-west Ulster; these
works were reprinted in one volume in 1978 as *Roots of
Presbyterianism in Donegal.*

Mention should also be made of unpublished histories of congregations, some of which may be found in archives and also online. A few examples are given here. In 1819–20 Alexander McMaster prepared a history of First Antrim (then known as Millrow) of which he was secretary (D2930/9/3). A remarkable work of the early nineteenth century is 'Historical Accounts of the Presbyterian Congregations of Ballynahinch, Dromara, Kilmore and Drumcaw now Clough, all in the County of Down, Ireland, with a transcript from the original Registers of the Congregation of Ballynahinch from the 21st August 1696 to 1734' by the brothers, John Strong Armstrong and Rev. James Armstrong, minister of Strand Street, Dublin (CR3/69).[18]

Among the papers of Rev. William Kennedy McKay in PRONI is 'The History of Carland Congregation from its first establishment in 1648 to 1826' (D2594/2A–F). The Johnston Central Library in Cavan Town has a copy of Thomas Hall's unpublished study, 'The history of Presbyterianism in East Cavan and a small portion of Meath and Monaghan' (1912).[19] The Ulster Museum has a catalogue reference (Acc. 61–1949) to a history of Newtowncrommelin Presbyterian Church by John Stewart (1947).[20] Further information of relevance may be found in the Presbyterian Historical Society's folders of material on individual congregations, comprising newspaper cuttings, leaflets, orders of service, etc.

Notes

[1] From the Preface to his *Historical Essay on the Parish and Congregation of Templepatrick* (1825).

[2] Blair, *Kilraughts*, p. 49.

[3] *RGSU*, vol. 1, p. 432.

[4] Holmes, *Our Irish Presbyterian Heritage*, p. 116.

[5] *Belfast and Ulster Directory, 1900.*

[6] McKinney, *Killinchy*, p. 45.

[7] Wylie, *Terrace Row ... Coleraine*, pp 15–19.

[8] Kilpatrick, *Claggan*, pp 11–12.

[9] Neill, *Castlederg*, p. 18. See *Parish Boundaries: Presbyterian Church in Ireland*, printed at 'The Witness' Office, Royal Avenue, Belfast, 1917. It is

interesting that the word 'parish' is used here in the context of defining the boundaries of congregations. Whatever Presbyterians meant by parish, it ought not to be confused with the parish systems used by the state, the Church of Ireland and the Roman Catholic Church.

10 Fisher, *Albany*, p. 7.

11 Mullin, *New Row … Coleraine*, p. 27.

12 Kilpatrick, *Third Rathfriland*, p. 7.

13 There was an earlier *History of Congregations*, prepared by W. D. Killen and published in 1886, though this looked only at the congregations of the Synod of Ulster.

14 *RGSU*, vol. 3, p. 511.

15 Sherrard, *Ballylinney*, p. 14.

16 *On the Meeting House Steps … Stewartstown*, pp 77–9.

17 McClelland, *Clare*.

18 Also available online at https://rosdavies.com and in the members' area of the UHF website (www.ancestryireland.com).

19 This has been made available on the library's website.

20 See also *Belfast Telegraph*, 20 January 1948; Eull Dunlop, 'Master John Stewart of Newtowncrommelin: a local historical parable', *The Glynns*, vol. 30 (2002), pp 93–100.

3

Presbyterians and their records

Many of the presbyteries and Kirk Sessions preserve full and valuable Records. ... If any experiment at forming local offices be tried, I would suggest an effort to gather the Records of the Presbyterian Churches, say at Belfast.

John Mills, Deputy Keeper of the Records, Dublin, 1900[1]

3.1 Presbyterian record-keeping

The creation of records is an inherent characteristic of Presbyterianism wherever it is found. In part this is a reflection of the nature of Presbyterianism itself, with its different layers of church government arising from the key concept of accountability. There is little difference in the types of record generated by the historic Presbyterian denominations in Ireland, though there may be occasional variations in emphasis. Genealogists have long recognised that the registers of baptisms and marriages maintained by individual churches are among the most important documents for studying Presbyterian families. However, many other records were generated by congregations, including minute and account books, financial reports and rolls of members. The higher courts of Presbyterian church government have also generated copious amounts of documentation, which can be helpful for those seeking details on their forebears. These subjects are dealt with in more detail in the chapters which follow. This chapter provides a general introduction to Presbyterian records and where they may be found in Ireland.

At the outset it should be acknowledged that while the different categories of church records (e.g. baptisms, marriages, minutes and accounts) are discussed individually in the following chapters, it does not mean that they are all found in separate books. It is often the case that the same volume can contain a range of records, i.e. a single book might contain baptisms and marriages, as well as minutes of meetings. This is especially true of early records. The following description of the earliest volume of records of Antrim Presbyterian Church was penned by Rev. W. S. Smith in 1899:

> This is a book 8½ inches long by 6½ wide, and 1 inch in thickness. 54 pages were devoted to marriages (6 pages are missing), and 119 pages to baptisms. ... The old book also contains a number of miscellaneous entries; some it may be of an official, and others of a very unofficial, character; but of considerable interest nevertheless. The period covered by the combined baptismal and marriage entries is about sixty years, from 1674 till 1736, though there are only several entries after 1733. Most of the miscellaneous entries, excepting such as refer to ministers, are from forty to fifty years later. After serving the purpose of a congregational register, it was made to do duty as a petty cash-book in connection with the distribution of congregational charity and the cultivation of the congregational land.[2]

The above paragraph was from an article by Smith in the *Ulster Journal of Archaeology* and was penned at a time that there was a deepening interest in identifying and preserving historical records, including documents relating to Presbyterianism. Smith's own sense of excitement at handling this volume, which he noted was 'in a very fair state of preservation' despite its age, comes through clearly:

> The paper is thick, and much darkened by time. It is bound in leather; the covers being ornamented with impressed diamond-shaped figures, enclosed in bordering lines. It is a book to exercise somewhat of a magical influence over the imagination, transporting one into the past, to live in other times, to think new thoughts, and to witness other scenes.

The challenge for Smith, as countless genealogists and historians have contended with, was deciphering the ancient handwriting and orthography:

> Though interesting to look into, the writing in certain portions of it is very puzzling. In some parts it is beautiful even now, while the diction is embellished with a few Latin expressions. In others the

writing is coarse and angular, the letters being like multitudes of beetles' legs strewn over the pages until they are almost black, and the spelling such that would have astonished the late Sir Isaac Pitman.[3] To decipher these letters at all freely is impossible to anyone not familiar with such writing. Even the same word is not always spelled alike by the same hand. Indeed, spelling with most of the recording officials (and they must have been fairly numerous) was a matter of the most sublime indifference. The name William, for instance, is spelled in three different ways in as many lines; while Donegore, a neighbouring parish, is spelled in ten different ways; but these extend over a good number of years. Many family names are spelled phonetically, while others are given in the most round-about fashion.

Smith's article was one of a number to appear in antiquarian journals at this time, with other essays considering the early records of Armagh, Banbridge, Carnmoney, Dundonald, Lisburn and Templepatrick.[4] Other important initiatives included the publication of the minutes of the meetings of the General Synod of Ulster from 1691 to 1820 in three volumes.[5] This work had been undertaken by a Committee for Historical Purposes, which had been set up by the General Assembly following a request from the Presbyterian Historical Society of America in 1877 for books and documents of interest. There was as yet, however, no central repository for the records of Irish Presbyterianism.

3.2 Presbyterian Historical Society of Ireland

The impetus to identify and preserve materials of historical importance for future generations gathered pace in the early years of the twentieth century. Alexander G. Crawford of Coleraine was one of a number of people to highlight the importance of safeguarding the records of Irish Presbyterianism. During a trip to the United States Crawford had visited the offices of the American Presbyterian Historical Society in Philadelphia and was impressed with what he saw. In a letter to the *Northern Whig* in June 1905 he called for the formation of a similar society in Ireland with rooms in the new Assembly Buildings in Belfast. This finally sparked action and over the next two years, with the support of the General Assembly and the other branches of Irish Presbyterianism, the idea of a society became a reality. In January 1907 a room was acquired in Assembly Buildings and in May of that year a constitution for the Presbyterian Historical Society of Ireland was approved.[6]

Very quickly the Society built up a significant collection of books and documents, some of which travelled some distance to the Society's Library or emerged from unusual places. The early donations to the Library included, thanks to Captain Richard Linn of New Zealand, copies of two eighteenth-century registers of Banbridge Presbyterian Church.[7] The earliest surviving register of Killyleagh Presbyterian Church, covering the years 1693–1756, was presented to the Society by the Dowager Marchioness of Dufferin and Ava of Clandeboye House, near Bangor. Once described as a 'Treasure House of Ulster's History', the Society's library and archive possesses upwards of 12,000 books and pamphlets. Naturally, these are mainly concerned with ecclesiastical history and in particular Presbyterianism, with an excellent collection of congregational histories. In addition the Society holds significant manuscript collections, ranging from the records of individual congregations to the personal papers of ministers and missionaries. The Society also has a duplicate set of PRONI's microfilms of Presbyterian congregational records. A range of Presbyterian artefacts, including an extensive collection of Communion tokens, as well as Communion plate and portraits, is in the Society's possession.

The Society's early *Annual Reports* and *Proceedings* contain a wealth of information on manuscripts accessioned and include biographical sketches of historical figures, as well as extracts from documents and other genealogical material. For example, the *Annual Report for 1908* lists the names of tenants on Sir Robert McClelland's estate in north County Londonderry in the early 1600s (which helpfully includes their place of origin in Scotland); the original documents from which the names have been extracted were in what was then HM General Register House, Edinburgh (now the National Records of Scotland). The same report includes the transcription of a 'call' issued by the congregation in Coleraine in 1673, including the names of subscribers, taken from the Wodrow Manuscripts in the National Library of Scotland. These publications are in PHSI, while PRONI also has some of them (CR3/46/11). Nearly every year since 1970 the Society has published a *Bulletin*, which includes articles on different aspects of Presbyterian history and book reviews. The Society's website (www.presbyterianhistoryireland.com) includes a significant amount of material of value to historians and genealogists and is referred to frequently throughout this book.

A specific task that the General Assembly entrusted to the Presbyterian Historical Society was the creation of a Roll of Honour of Presbyterians who had served, and in many cases had died, in the First World War. This was published in 1921 as *The Presbyterian Church in Ireland. Roll of Honour 1914–1919*, copies of which are available in PHSI, PRONI (CR3/46/7/1) and many libraries. The Roll of Honour is arranged by presbytery and congregation and provides the name and address of the serviceman, his rank, and his regiment, battalion or unit. For many of those listed additional remarks are included, such as 'wounded', 'killed in action', 'prisoner of war' or 'decorated'. Inevitably there are gaps, but the Roll of Honour is a remarkable record of over 24,000 names including over 4,000 names of those who died. Also listed are ministers and their sons and daughters who served.[8] The Roll of Honour is available as a searchable database on the PHSI website (members only).

3.3 Public Record Office of Northern Ireland

The other major archive for Irish Presbyterian records is the Public Record Office of Northern Ireland (PRONI) in Titanic Quarter, Belfast. One of the main features of the documentary collections in PRONI is the fact that they cover both public (i.e. official) and private records. Furthermore, PRONI's holdings of private records include documentation for not just Northern Ireland, but for the entire province of Ulster and further afield. Many of PRONI collections have been catalogued in some detail and the information in its once voluminous paper catalogues is now available electronically via the institution's online eCatalogue. Of great value for genealogists is the huge collection of church records of all of the major religious denominations, including the different branches of Presbyterianism. In one format or another, PRONI has records for most of the Presbyterian congregations in all nine counties of Ulster, as well as some from other parts of Ireland. These are mainly available on microfilm (as noted above, the PHSI has a duplicate set of these), though there are also many original records as well as photocopies of originals.

In recent times PRONI has been making some church records available in-house (not online) in digital format. For instance, PRONI now has digital copies of the records of Dundonald Presbyterian Church, including a book containing minutes of Session meetings as well as baptisms and marriages, *c.* 1678–1716 (CR3/79). Other collections of particular relevance to those researching Presbyterians and Presbyterianism include the antiquarian and genealogical papers of Rev. David Stewart, a highly energetic office-holder in the Presbyterian Historical Society, which are catalogued under reference D1759 (now microfilmed with reference MIC637); these include many transcripts of Presbyterian records, as well as extensive notes on families, with a particular focus on County Down.[9]

3.4 Guides to records in PRONI and PHSI

First published in hard copy format in 1994 and now available as an electronic resource, the *Guide to Church Records* created by PRONI is the starting point for enquiring into the availability of records for individual Presbyterian congregations in the Public Record Office of Northern Ireland. The *Guide* can be downloaded as a PDF from PRONI's website. The arrangement of churches and their records in the *Guide* is by civil parish and Presbyterian congregations are listed under the parish in which the meeting house is located. The catchment area of a Presbyterian congregation is not of course limited by the boundaries of a civil parish and so researchers should bear in mind that while a Presbyterian place of worship may have been in a particular parish, those who gathered there may have travelled from neighbouring parishes.

Taking Aghadowey Presbyterian Church as an example, the *Guide to Church Records* indicates that the following records are available for this congregation:

Minutes of Session Meetings, 1702–61	Digital Records – CR3/80
Baptisms, 1855–1944; marriages, 1845–1923; committee minutes, 1851–85; stipend lists, 1832–54; Communion rolls, 1903–13.	MIC1P/123
Session minutes, 1702–61	In Presbyterian Historical Society

It will be seen that the original volume of eighteenth-century Session minutes, which is on deposit in the Presbyterian Historical Society, has now been digitised by PRONI and can be viewed there. The other listed records of this congregation, including baptisms and marriages, can be viewed on microfilm in PRONI.

PRONI's *Guide to Church Records* includes details on records available for some churches, including Presbyterian congregations, in counties outside of Ulster. Some of these records can be viewed on microfilm in PRONI, such as those for Clontarf, which include baptisms and marriages beginning in 1836 (at this time the congregation's meeting house was in Lower Gloucester Street in the city of Dublin) as well as Session and committee minutes and a stipend book (MIC1P/430). Other records for congregations in southern counties listed in the *Guide to Church Records* are available in the Presbyterian Historical Society. These include, for example, records of the Presbyterian Church in Waterford from 1826 onwards. The *Guide to Church Records'* listing of congregational records held by the Presbyterian Historical Society is incomplete. However, the PHSI has added downloadable PDFs of congregational records – arranged by county for Ulster and province for the rest of Ireland – to its website, which contain a much fuller listing of items in its custody.

3.5 Other archives and libraries in Greater Belfast

The Gamble Library of Union Theological College has a vast collection of books, pamphlets and manuscripts relating to the story of Irish Presbyterianism. These include records of some individual congregations as well as minutes of the higher courts of the Church; the Presbyterian Mission Archive is also available here. There is a small Historical Library in the Reformed Theological College at Knockbracken, just outside Belfast, which for the most part contains publications and other printed materials, such as minutes of the Reformed Presbyterian Synod. The Special Collections at Queen's University Belfast include the Allen Collection (MS 23), comprising the papers of two respected historians of Presbyterianism, Rev. Robert Allen (1904–68) and Rev. W. T. Latimer (1842–1919), and the Antrim Presbytery Collection which contains literary, philosophical and theological volumes mainly published before 1800 that were acquired by non-subscribing congregations in Belfast and Antrim.

The holdings of the Ulster Museum include a few items of interest, including several eighteenth-century 'calls' to ministers named Kennedy (see Chapter 7).

Of other institutions in Belfast, attention can be drawn to the Linen Hall Library, founded in 1788 as the Belfast Reading Society. The Library's Blackwood Collection includes a list of members (1851) of Clough Non-Subscribing Presbyterian Church, County Down, transcribed from the original manuscript in the possession of James Watson, Ballymacreely, by Reginald W. H. Blackwood in 1933.[10] The Randal Gill Library of the North of Ireland Family History Society, located in Newtownabbey a few miles north of Belfast, has a large collection of transcriptions of church registers, including many for Presbyterian congregations. This library also holds on permanent loan the genealogical correspondence of the Presbyterian Historical Society. This extensive collection of letters and envelopes has been catalogued and indexes are available on the NIFHS website (www.nifhs.org). Nearly 4,000 names are mentioned, though the information available on each one varies considerably.

3.6 Archives and libraries in the Republic of Ireland

For the availability of records relating to congregations in Dublin, Steven Smyrl's *Dictionary of Dublin Dissent* (2009) is indispensible. The author lists the surviving records for each congregation and indicates where these are available. Many of them remain in local custody, though some are in publicly accessible archives and libraries. The original records of a congregation of the Presbyterian Church of Wales in Talbot Street, Dublin, are in the Anglesey Archives in Wales. However, there are computerised indexes to baptisms (1839–1923) and marriages (1892–1936) in the Gilbert Library in Dublin. The Royal Irish Academy (RIA) in Dublin holds the vast Dublin Unitarian Church Collection. The Unitarian Church in St Stephen's Green descends from the congregations of Wood Street, Cook Street, Eustace Street, and Strand Street, which belonged to the non-subscribing Synod of Munster. The collection was deposited on two separate occasions, in 2006 and 2008, and has been catalogued in full (the very detailed catalogue may be downloaded from the RIA website (www.ria.ie)).

Congregational records can also be found in a number of other public institutions in the Republic of Ireland. For instance, records relating to Dundalk Presbyterian Church, covering the years 1839–1923, are on deposit in the National Library of Ireland (NLI) in Dublin and include financial records, minute books, and records relating to the church library (MS 33,682). Papers of the clerical Bruce family are also held here (MSS 20,867–21,961), including a register of marriages and baptisms performed by Rev. William Bruce at Lisburn, 1779–80, 1782 (MS 20,891), and a register of marriages conducted in Belfast and vicinity by him, 1790–1801 (MS 20,892). Another of the documents of interest in NLI is a petition of 1829 to King George IV concerning Catholic Emancipation by the Secession congregation of 'Leacumpher' (Lecumpher) signed by the minister, Rev. James Wilson, and many members (MS 50,660).

The Manuscripts & Archives Research Library at Trinity College Dublin has some documents of interest, including late eighteenth-century diaries that have been attributed to Rev. William Bruce (see Chapter 7). The Genealogical Office, a department of the National Library of Ireland, has a copy of the diary of Rev. Adam Blair (1718–90), a non-subscribing minister (GO, MS 544). Records can turn up in unusual places. For example, a collection of records of John A. Traynor, auctioneer and insurance agent in Carlow, now in the National Archives of Ireland, includes an account book for the Presbyterian Church in Carlow (known as the 'Scots Church'), covering the period from the early 1840s to 1895 (BR CAR 1).

The Louth County Archives Service, based in Dundalk, has an extensive collection of records for the congregations of Dundalk and Carlingford (including Greenore and Omeath) and others for the congregations of Castlebellingham and Jonesboro' (PP00075). The items include account books, communicants' rolls, minute books and correspondence; the records for Dundalk complement the documents noted above on deposit in the National Library of Ireland. The Cork City and County Archives has several collections of Presbyterian records. These include Cork Presbyterian Meeting House Account Books, 1758–1822 (CCCA/U025), concerning the congregation in Princes Street (now the Unitarian Church), and the Richard Dowden Papers (CCCA/U140); Dowden (1794–1861) was for many years the treasurer and a trustee of this church. The Cork repository also possesses two minute books of the committee responsible for maintaining the building and finances of the former

'Scots Church' in Cobh (formerly Queenstown and before that Cove), 1841–60, 1867–1953 (CCCA/U100).

3.7 Keeping an open mind

One point to emphasise is that it is vitally important to keep an open mind on the religious affiliation of one's ancestors. They may well have been devout Presbyterians, but that does not mean that they will be found exclusively in records generated by Presbyterian churches. It cannot be overstated that research into Presbyterian ancestors should not be restricted to Presbyterian records. It is especially important to take into consideration Church of Ireland registers of baptisms, marriages and burials. Until 1 January 1871 the Church of Ireland was the established or state church in Ireland and at least in part due to its status many people who ordinarily belonged to another denomination can turn up in the pages of its registers. For instance, the following curious entry appears in the register of Antrim Church of Ireland:

> Robert Harley, a Glover in Antrim, of the Established Church married to a presbyterian wife, had his child, born this year [1737], baptised by Mr Dougal, a presbyterian minister, said Harley pretending he gave way to it because he could not get coffins (MIC1/328/1).

The records of Ballymore Church of Ireland, County Armagh, include a list of Presbyterians baptised, 1822–31. Many Presbyterians will be found in Church of Ireland burial registers. For example, the register of St Nicholas's Church, Carrickfergus, records the burial on 19 August 1748 of Rev. James Fraizer, 'Dissenting Teacher of Carrickfergus'; the funeral was conducted by the curate, Rev. Thomas Finley. The Armoy Church of Ireland burial register includes an entry from 1858 of a John Ferris who was described as a 'Protestant dissenter of the Covenanters. A United Irishman in the rebellion of 1798 and twice narrowly escaped being hanged' (MIC1/334).

Local practices could also result in the offspring of Presbyterians being baptised in the Church of Ireland. The Ordnance Survey Memoir of Island Magee, County Antrim, completed in 1840, includes the following interesting comment in a discussion of illegitimacy in the parish: 'All children being born before or immediately after marriage, though of Presbyterian parents, are brought for baptism to the [Church of Ireland] rector.'[11] The registers of other Protestant denominations should also be considered and even Catholic records should not be discounted in the search for Presbyterian forebears. Catholic baptism and marriage registers occasionally include references to Presbyterians who had converted to Catholicism. For example, the baptism register of St Peter's Catholic Church in Belfast includes an entry for 6 November 1867 concerning Letitia Creely, daughter of John Gawdy and Mary Eiken. Her year of birth was entered as 1780 and there was an additional note that she was an 87-year-old Presbyterian convert, whose parents had been Presbyterians.

The keeping of an open mind on the religious affiliation of one's ancestors should also extend to the different branches of Presbyterianism. As the records reveal time and again, people switched between the Presbyterian denominations for many different reasons, including theological and personal. Researchers should also be mindful of the origins of the congregation to which their ancestors belonged and should consider whether the church was founded as the result of a congregational or denominational split. For example, in 1835 the minister of Killinchy Presbyterian Church, Rev. Samuel Watson, joined the Remonstrant Synod (which eventually became part of the Non-Subscribing Presbyterian Church). Not all of the members agreed with Watson, however, which in the end resulted in the creation of two separate congregations. The pre-1835 records of the church (including baptisms and marriages from 1812/13 and accounts going back to the early 1780s) were retained by the minister or one of his supporters (CR4/17; D1759/1/D; MIC637/3). Therefore, although counted among the records of Killinchy Non-Subscribing Presbyterian Church, they do in fact concern all Presbyterians in the Killinchy area prior to the split.

3.8 The absence of records

Sadly, not all records have survived to the present day. Some records perished accidentally as the following extract from the baptismal register of West Church, Ballymena, records:

> I preached at Churchtown on the 5th of November 1848 according to appointment by Presbytery and the list of children baptised on that

day having been accidentally destroyed in my absence, I am necessitated to leave blank in the register at the same time noting its cause (MIC1P/105).

Due to the 'negligence and disobedience of a female servant' some of the records of Bready Reformed Presbyterian Church were lost in a fire in the home of the Clerk of Session in September 1868.[12] Other records were destroyed deliberately. The Session book of Convoy Reformed Presbyterian Church has a gap between 1874 and 1891 and the following comment has been added to the minutes: 'Some person with evil design and reckless abandon removed the missing records, and one feels utterly unable to understand the motives that directed such a vile action to outrage justice and stifle truth.' The records of the Presbyterian congregation that met in Union Chapel in Lower Abbey Street in Dublin were destroyed during the Easter Rising of 1916. Having been deposited in the Public Record Office of Ireland in 1921, the registers of baptisms and marriages of Plunket Street Presbyterian Church in Dublin, 1672–1766, perished in the destruction of that archive in 1922. The baptismal records of Rosemary Street Presbyterian Church, 1868–1941, were destroyed as a result of a German air raid during the Second World War.

Occasionally, registers disappeared around the time that a minister died or moved to a new congregation. This may also have occurred if a Clerk of Session retired or passed away. The Session book for Larne and Kilwaughter includes a minute from 1721 in which, after noting that Robert Robinson had given up the position of Clerk, recorded, 'Mr Robinson's minutes are not to be found.'[13] Following the death of the Treasurer and Clerk of Session of Malone Presbyterian Church, Belfast, in the early part of the twentieth century, 'for two days a man carried papers out of his house to the garden, where they were reduced to ashes'.[14] A ministerial vacancy could also account for a gap in the records, or even a period of illness for the minister.

On other occasions record-keeping was simply lax. In both the baptismal and marriage registers of First Donegore there is a gap between 1813 and 1819. The reason for this was due to the fact that 'Mr Cooke neglected continuing the register' (MIC/1P/79). Mr Cooke was the famous Rev. Dr Henry Cooke who was minister of the congregation from 1811 to 1818. He is regarded as a major figure in the Presbyterian Church in the nineteenth century and it is somewhat surprising that he should have been remiss when it came to record-keeping when he was punctilious on so many other matters. The comment on his failure to maintain the register was made by his successor, Rev. James Seaton Reid, one of the greatest historians of the Presbyterian Church. Cooke was not alone in this. In the 1830s one of the charges laid against the minister of the Secession congregation in Moneymore, County Londonderry, was that he failed to keep records adequately.[15]

In some congregations there is, sadly, a dearth of records from before the second half of the nineteenth century. In his history of the Presbyterian churches in Donagheady parish Rev. John Rutherford noted that a visitation of First Donagheady in 1860, when the minister was Rev. John Roulstone, found that there was no committee book or communicants' roll. He continued:

> At a visitation held five years later it was stated that there was no Baptismal Register, no Communicants' Roll and no books in which to record the proceedings of the Kirk Session and Committee. In 1871 it was reported that there was only one book for baptisms, Communicants' Roll and Session records. In 1876 it was reported that there was no Minutes of any Committee Meeting held since 1871. Mr Roulstone, though not wholly, was chiefly responsible for this negligence. It was not until 1878 that a Baptismal Register was provided and no record of any baptism in connection with the congregation prior to that date is now available. Some of the entries are without a date, some are incomplete, in some the writing is illegible, and there are many omissions. In the same year a Committee Book was provided, but only one or two entries were made in it during his ministry.[16]

The absence of records has presented challenges for those writing congregational histories. Rev. Thomas Boyd began a history of the congregation in Banbridge in which he had served for many years with the lament, 'In compiling a history of Scarva Street Presbyterian church one is met at the outset by the paucity of information available. The Congregational Records are few and imperfect.'[17] When Jack Johnston began work on a history of Glenhoy Presbyterian Church in the Clogher Valley of County Tyrone he had to contend with the fact that there were no records of baptisms before

1864, no marriage registers before 1907, no committee minutes before 1917, and no Session minutes before 1944.[18] These gaps are also deeply frustrating for genealogical researchers. The story is told that opponents of Andrew Jackson travelled to Ireland from America in search of evidence that he had been born here and so was ineligible for the Presidency. On making their way to Carrickfergus, the home place of Jackson's parents, they looked up the register of the Presbyterian Church only to find that the relevant pages were missing and so no evidence was found, one way or another, of Jackson's baptism.[19]

Notes

[1] *Report of the Committee Appointed to Enquire as to the Existing Arrangements for the Collection and Custody of Local Records* (1902), p. 256.

[2] W. S. Smith, 'Early register of the old Presbyterian congregation of Antrim', *UJA*, 2nd series, vol. 5 (Sept. 1899), p. 180.

[3] A nineteenth-century educator and inventor of a system of shorthand based on phonetics.

[4] 'A list of Presbyterian marriages copied from the Session-Book of the Congregation of Armagh, 1707–28', *JRSAI*, 5th series, vol. 8 (1898), pp 345–51; Richard Linn and W. T. Latimer, 'Marriage Register of the Presbyterian Congregation of Banbridge, County Down, 1756–1794', *JRSAI*, 5th series, vol. 39 (1909), pp 75–84; William Fee McKinney, 'Old session books of Carnmoney, County Antrim, 1686–1821', *UJA*, 2nd series, vol. 6 (Jan. 1900), pp 6–11; 'The old session book of the Presbyterian congregation at Dundonald', *UJA*, 2nd series, vol. 3 (July 1893), pp 227–32; vol. 4 (Oct. 1897), pp 33–66; 'Session books of first Lisburn Presbyterian congregation', *UJA*, 2nd series, vol. 6 (1900), p. 183; 'The old session-book of Templepatrick Presbyterian Church', edited by W. T. Latimer, *JRSAI*, 5th series, vol. 5 (1895), pp 130–34; vol. 11 (1901), pp 162–75, 259–72.

[5] *Records of the General Synod of Ulster*, 3 vols (1890–98).

[6] Joseph Thompson, *Times Passing: The Story of the Presbyterian Historical Society of Ireland from 1907* (2007).

[7] Linn was a native of Banbridge and was engaged writing a history of the town at the time of his death in 1911; this was eventually published in 1935 as *A History of Banbridge*, edited by W. S. Kerr.

8 The Roll of Honour lists 41 ministers who served as chaplains. See Victor Dobbin, 'Chaplaincy in the First World War', *BPHSI*, vol. 38 (2014).

9 See also a scrapbook of letters from Rev. David Stewart, Belfast, of the Presbyterian Historical Society regarding genealogical material, 1937–51 (D3815/A/350).

10 The original of this volume is in PRONI (D3694/D/3/2).

11 *Ordnance Survey Memoirs of Ireland Vol. 10: Parishes of County Antrim III: Larne and Island Magee* (1991), p. 37.

12 Roulston, *Foyle Valley Covenanters*, p. 6.

13 Porter, *Larne and Kilwaughter*, p. 53.

14 Robb, *Malone*, p. 155.

15 *History of Congregations*, p. 651.

16 Rutherford, *Donagheady*, p. 53.

17 Boyd, *Scarva Street*, p. 9.

18 Johnston, *Glenhoy*, pp 11, 37.

19 *Donahoe's Magazine*, vol. 27 (1892), p. 115.

4

Registers of baptisms and marriages

Resolved that a Registry Book be kept in the Congregation of all Marriages and Baptisms here, pursuant to an Act of Synod. That a Sum not less than Sixpence for each Child Baptized, and a Sum not less than One Shilling for each Marriage, be paid to the Clerk for his Trouble for making the Proper Entries ...

Carrickfergus committee, 11 Nov. 1819[1]

4.1 Presbyterians and baptism

Presbyterians practise infant baptism, and the registers of these baptisms form one of the most useful categories of record when looking for ancestors, especially in the period prior to the introduction of civil registration of births in 1864. The circumstances in which baptism was administered varied over time and between Presbyterian denominations and congregations. According to the 1645 *Directory for the Publick Worship of God*, baptism was to be administered publicly and the child was to be presented for baptism by the father (or a suitable person if the father could not do so). Despite the stipulation that baptisms should take place in a public setting, the practice of private baptism became prevalent. There were periodic attempts to curb this. For example, in 1718 the Presbytery of Strabane heard complaints from some ministers of the 'unreasonable fateigues & inconveniences they are exposed to by baptizing children privately'; in response the Presbytery ruled that private baptisms should be avoided if possible (CR3/26/2/1). In practice, however, by the early nineteenth century it was more usual for baptisms to take place in the family home. In some areas at least baptisms were times of communal celebration. The Ordnance Survey Memoir for Donegore parish, County Antrim, of 1838–9 recorded that baptisms were 'occasions of mirth and feasting, the family usually inviting as many "sitters" (as the guests are termed) as the house can accommodate.'[2]

In the early 1800s there were moves in some congregations to limit the occurrence of private baptisms. The Session of First Dunboe agreed in 1809 that baptisms should be administered in public since this was 'agreeable to the divine Word, to our form of church government, [and] to the directory for public worship'; the minister, however, was allowed the discretion to perform private baptisms 'in peculiar circumstances'. In addition, it was 'earnestly requested' by the Session that no member should seek baptism in situations 'which by refusing could cause offence and division.[3] In 1818 the Secession congregation of Loughaghery, County Down, set down a series of specific conditions for private baptisms, including if the family lived more than two miles from the meeting house. In 1820 the following rule appeared in a new set of regulations agreed in Millisle:

> ... the Minister and Session desire to express their unwillingness that children should be baptised on the Sabbath in private houses except to persons who are servants themselves to others, and in cases of absolute necessity. The minister is willing to baptize children each Sabbath publicly in the meeting-house, but he considers the collection of friends which sometimes takes place at a baptism, and the conversation that commonly occurs, inconsistent with the sanctification of the Sabbath, nor will he continue to baptize children to such parents as willingly neglect the observance of the Sacrament of the Lord's Supper, or Public Worship.[4]

There were further moves towards public baptism in the 1830s. In 1834 the Session of May Street Presbyterian Church, Belfast, agreed that baptisms would take place publicly on the first Sunday of each month, while in 1836 the Synod of Ulster recommended public baptism.[5] It is clear, however, that many baptisms continued to take place in the home and on days other than Sunday. This may have been more common in rural congregations where many families lived some distance from the place of worship. Some ministers baptised infants as they conducted pastoral visitation of the families in their congregations. This was the practice of Rev. Thomas Beare of Drumreagh Presbyterian Church; usually he baptised two or three children on the days set aside for visitation, though on Friday, 8 September 1865 he managed to baptise seven children in six different townlands.[6] In 1846 the Session of Maghera issued an unusual ruling when asked to baptise privately two children of John Black: it was agreed that the older child could be baptised in private if the younger was baptised in public.[7] In the late 1880s Rev. Robert Parke, minister of Third Ramelton, recorded the venue for the baptism in the register, usually providing a justification if the ceremony did not take place in the church, e.g. 'child poorly', 'mother poorly' and 'by leave of Session' (MIC1P/209).

Typically the father presented the child for baptism, though where, for whatever reason (e.g. death, under church censure, out of the country), this was not possible the mother, grandfather or another appointed individual could stand in for him. Baptism was usually limited to the children of members or adherents of the congregation. Full communicant membership was generally not a prerequisite, though in some congregations it was insisted upon. In some churches access to baptism was linked to having a seat in the meeting house. In 1820 the congregation of Millisle issued instructions that before anyone could have a child baptised the name of that person had to be entered in the 'seat book'. Those who were not full members of the congregation had to apply to Session to have their offspring baptised.[8] The Carnmoney Session ruled in 1847 that persons seeking baptism for their children who were not already seatholders had to take one-quarter of a seat in the 'Little Aisle' of the meeting house or pay £0 2s. 6d. to the treasurer each year.[9]

4.2 Registers of baptisms

Although there are some very early Presbyterian registers of baptism, including Antrim (1677), Lisburn (1692), Killyleagh (1693), Drumbo (1699), and Portaferry (1699), in the majority of cases, baptismal records do not pre-date the nineteenth century. This may be for the very simple reason that the congregation was not established until the 1800s, though the issues with record-keeping discussed above were also factors. Late seventeenth- and eighteenth-century registers come in different formats. The catchment area for the congregation of Larne and Kilwaughter was quite large and the baptisms are divided into sections each covering a particular geographical area: Kilwaughter, the New Town of Larne, the Old Town of Larne, the parish of 'Glen' (Glynn), and the parish of

'Ralow' (Raloo). This register also includes a list of people who had children baptised and did not pay the clerk's dues (MIC1B/6).

The earliest surviving record of baptisms in the First Presbyterian Church in Belfast is titled, 'Register of Births in the old congregation of Protestant Dissenters in Belfast commencing April the first 1756'.[10] Though in many instances the date of baptism has been included, it is, as the title indicates, primarily a record of births. In his analysis of the register Alexander Gordon observes: 'Up to the year 1790, the entries were made, after the baptism, either by the sexton or by the parent, and are often exceedingly illiterate. From 6th May, 1790, the entries were made by the minister.' He notes that the register cannot be considered a complete record of the births in families belonging to the congregation, observing that between 6 May and 4 July 1790 only two baptisms are entered, compared with 11 that the minister himself recorded in this same period.

Many Presbyterian baptismal registers begin in 1819 or shortly thereafter for at the meeting of the Synod of Ulster in that year the following instructions were issued:

> That every minister of the Synod be enjoined to register, or cause to be registered, in a book to be kept for that purpose, the names of all children baptised by him; the dates of their birth and baptism; the names of their parents, and the places of residence. This book shall be carefully preserved, and considered as the property of the congregation – to remain with them on the death, resignation, or removal of the Minister, and to be handed to his Successor, for the purpose of continuing the registry.[11]

The minister was to have charge of the register unless there was a vacancy when it would be looked after by the Clerk of Session.

The range of information recorded in a baptismal register can vary quite considerably. Early registers may only provide the date of baptism, the name of the child and the name of the father. Occasionally the name of the child is not even recorded. A comment in the eighteenth-century Larne and Kilwaughter register explains why this was so in that congregation: 'Note that many of the blanks for children's names in this book are their being private baptisms and the children's names not told to me.' Later on the information recorded became much fuller. In the early 1800s Rev. Robert Magill of First Antrim recorded the name of the child, the date of birth as well as the date of baptism, the name of both parents (including the mother's maiden name), and the family's place of residence. Not every minister at this stage was as thorough as Magill, but by the second half of the nineteenth century this level of detail became fairly standard.

Generally speaking, the baptism of a child took place within a few weeks or months of the date of birth. It was not unusual, however, for a baptism to take place years after the birth. For example, the register of First Antrim records that on 11 September 1820 six-year-old James and two-year-old Jane, children of John and Jane Kirkpatrick, were baptised. John Bryson of Ballyvoy was 15 when he was baptised according to the register of Kilbride Presbyterian Church; this was 'by desire of himself as well as his parents' (MIC1P/331). Even older was David Campbell who was baptised in Crossgar Presbyterian Church, County Londonderry, in 1888. The following note was appended to his entry in the register:

> This D. Campbell spent 21 years and 43 days in the Army (4 years in England, 1 in Scotland, 3 in Ireland, 12 years and 27 days in India) before his baptism. While in the Army he was an Episcopalian, having gone over from the Presbyterian Church like a great many others; when he got off he attended the Episcopal Church in Macosquin for some time, but he wrote on a letter asking me to baptise him which I did on sincere profession of his faith (MIC1P/409).

4.3 Presbyterians and marriage

Although not considered to be a sacrament, the institution of marriage held an important place within Presbyterianism. According to the abovementioned *Directory for the Publick Worship of God* of 1645, an intended marriage should be made known publicly by the minister on three Sundays (the proclamation of banns); parental consent was required for those underage or who were marrying for the first time; the marriage ceremony should be held in the place of public worship before witnesses; and the details of the marriage should be recorded in a book 'for the perusal of all whom it may concern.'

For much of the eighteenth century one of the main grievances of Presbyterians concerned the right of their ministers to conduct marriages and for these marriages to have legal standing in the eyes of the state. This had consequences not only for the married couple, but also for their children. In 1737 a relief act was passed in the Irish Parliament which acknowledged that marriages conducted by Presbyterian ministers were legally valid so long as the officiant and those wishing to marry had taken or were about to take the oaths prescribed in the Toleration Act of 1719. A further act passed in 1782 confirmed that marriages between Presbyterians, and performed by a Presbyterian minister, were of equal standing to those of the Church of Ireland. Whether or not a Presbyterian minister was entitled to conduct a marriage between a Presbyterian and a member of the Church of Ireland remained a grey area.

In the face of the civil and religious establishment's refusal to recognise marriages conducted by Presbyterian ministers for much of the eighteenth century, the Synod of Ulster issued rulings at different times to ensure that marriages conducted under its auspices were as 'regular' as possible. In 1701 the Synod reiterated the ruling in the 1645 *Directory* that banns should be proclaimed on three Sundays before the marriage took place. However, banns were never very popular with Presbyterians and it has been suggested that in order to avoid them some Presbyterians married by licence in the Established Church. At local level there was often a degree of laxity in ensuring that banns were proclaimed on the requisite number of days or that marriages were conducted publicly. Ministers who failed to follow the rules were liable for suspension and even dismissal. In the late eighteenth century and early nineteenth century there were several attempts to provide further clarity on the responsibilities of ministers when it came to conducting marriages, especially when it concerned persons not under their pastoral care or who were members of the Church of Ireland. In 1802 Synod ruled that marriages could take place after the proclamation of banns on one Sunday. A year later the proclamation of banns was made optional.

Members who married clandestinely, or without parental consent, or who sought the services of a clergyman who was not of the Presbyterian Church could expect to be disciplined (see the section on Session books in Chapter 5). Other couples resorted to 'buckle-beggars' – usually defrocked clergymen who conducted marriages without any official sanction. These individuals gave considerable trouble to the different Presbyterian denominations. The Larne and Kilwaughter marriage register includes the following comment of *c.* 1768: 'at this time the buckle beggars marriages goes on and few or not but what is married by Mr Willson of Ballyclare, a discarded Presbyterian minister'. The implication would seem to be that Willson's activities had a negative effect on the number of marriages conducted by the minister of Larne and Kilwaughter.

In 1770 Rev. Hugh McCracken, who had been minister of Badoney in County Tyrone settled in the Carrickfergus area and began to conduct marriages of young people 'without the consent of their parents or guardians'. Eventually, in 1775, McCracken was deposed from the ministry. He died the following year and was buried in St Nicholas's churchyard in Carrickfergus; in the Church of Ireland burial register he is described as 'the buckle beggar'. Another such individual in the late eighteenth century was Rev. William Reynolds, a Seceder minister in the Newry area, who was disowned by his presbytery in 1777 for performing irregular marriage ceremonies. Reynolds continued to conduct marriages as a 'buckle-beggar' until at least the early 1790s.

With regard to the venues for marriages conducted by Presbyterian ministers, prior to 1845 most marriages – in some congregations at least – seem to have been celebrated in places other than the meeting house. Rev. John Dill was minister of Carnmoney between May 1825 and his death in February 1841 and during this time he conducted 232 marriages, 126 of them in the manse. Of the rest, 72 took place at the home of the bride or groom and the remainder at the homes of family or friends or at inns and public houses. None, it would seem, took place in the Carnmoney meeting house.[12]

4.4 Civil registration of marriage

In the early 1840s there were a number of high profile legal cases in which the validity of marriages conducted by Presbyterian ministers was challenged in the courts. These cases centred on whether Presbyterian ministers had the right to marry a couple where one or both were of the Established Church (Church of Ireland). Since hundreds of couples were in this position there was considerable anxiety in many households across the north of Ireland especially. One case in particular brought matters to a head. In 1842 George Millis stood trial in Carrickfergus on a charge of bigamy. His defence was that his first marriage had no legal standing as it had been conducted by a Presbyterian minister. The case was referred to the higher courts, eventually reaching the House of Lords. The final outcome was the defendant's acquittal. The case provoked a furious reaction from Presbyterians who felt that their rights were again being assaulted by the Church of Ireland hierarchy.

The background to the case provides an insight into the way in which Presbyterian marriages were conducted at this time. The minister who had performed the original marriage was Rev. John Johnston of Tullylish, County Down. Johnston was a careful keeper of records and at a special meeting of the General Assembly of the Presbyterian Church in March 1842 he drew on a range of documents in setting out his version of events.[13] The first item that he produced was a letter of 7 January 1828 from the Church of Ireland vicar of Seapatrick parish, Rev. Francis Burrows, to the Presbyterian minister of Banbridge, Rev. James Davis. In this letter the Anglican clergyman stated that George Millis wanted Davis to conduct a marriage between him and Esther Graham, the latter a member of the Banbridge congregation; Burrows expressed his hope that Davis would accede to this request. However, as Davis was away at the time, the parties wishing to get married approached Johnston. Before going any further, the Tullylish minister sought permission from the principal elder of Davis's congregation, Andrew McClelland, who was happy to grant it. He then married Millis and Graham on 10 January in the presence of John Roney and John Anthony.

Johnston made two records of the marriage, one of which was a paper certificate containing the signatures of the two witnesses, and the other an entry in his 'large registry-book'[14] (which Johnston held in his hand as he addressed the meeting). In emphasising the importance of keeping proper records, Johnston told those gathered:

> Documents like them I have preserved for many years, so that I cannot only turn to the registry of marriages which I have solemnized, but to the grounds on which I have solemnized them, and I require certificates of parties being agreed, and all being right, from my own Elders, even in the marriages of my own people.

The campaign for fairness for Presbyterians in the realm of marriage law led to the passing of *An Act for Confirmation of Certain Marriages in Ireland* of 1843, which recognised that marriages conducted by Presbyterian ministers had the same legal standing as those performed by clergymen of the Established Church. This was followed by *An Act for Marriages in Ireland; and for Registering such Marriages* (the *Marriages (Ireland) Act* for short), which received royal assent on 9 August 1844.[15] This Act provided for the civil registration of all non-Catholic marriages, i.e. marriages conducted in Protestant churches and in newly created registry offices, from 1 April 1845 onwards. Henceforth, these marriages would be registered in a uniform manner. (It was not until 1864 that Catholic marriages were registered with the state.) A General Register Office, presided over by a Registrar-General, was created in Dublin to maintain a centralised record of registered marriages, with district registrars appointed at local level. In some detail the Act set out the regulations concerning Presbyterian marriages; the following paragraph is one of the sections relating to these unions:

> Marriages between parties, both of whom are Presbyterians, may be solemnized according to the forms used by Presbyterians, either by the licence of a Presbyterian minister, or by publication of banns, as hereinafter respectively mentioned, in meeting houses to be certified as hereinafter mentioned, between the hours of eight in the morning and two in the afternoon, with open doors, and in the presence of two or more credible witnesses; and marriages between parties, of whom one only is a Presbyterian may be solemnized according to the same forms, by such licence of a Presbyterian minister, in such meeting houses, between the same hours, with open doors, and in the presence of two or more credible witnesses; provided that in either case there be no lawful impediment to the marriage of such parties.

4.5 Registers of marriages

There are some surviving examples of very early Presbyterian marriage registers. Marriages for the congregation in Antrim survive from 1675, while those for Lisburn date from 1688. Presbyterian marriage registers from the late seventeenth century through to the early nineteenth century will often be limited to a date and the names of the bride and groom. The date can be the date the marriage was solemnised or the date(s) of the proclamation of banns – or both. The early register of Antrim Presbyterian Church adopts this format as this entry from 1698 demonstrates:

> A purpose of marriage betwixt James Hood and Martha Strain of this parish were proclaimed the 1st day of May for the 1st time, the

8th day of May for the last time, were married the 18th of the same month (MIC1P/3/1).

The following example from the Ballykelly register shows the role of the parents in sanctioning the marriage of their offspring:

> John Steel and Jean Aleson gave in there names to be proclaimed in ordeur to marriage, there parents & both the parties being content this 20th of December 1701 both of them in Ballykelly and were married ye 10th of Jenry 1701 [1702] (MIC1P/208).

An insight into the recording of Presbyterian marriages in the second half of the eighteenth century is provided by the register of Banbridge Presbyterian Church for the years 1756–94, a transcription of which was published in the *Journal of the Royal Society of Antiquaries of Ireland* in 1909.[16] The minister of the congregation throughout this period was Rev. Henry Jackson, who was joined by an assistant, Rev. Nathaniel Shaw, in 1790. The marriage entries up to 30 March 1761 begin 'A Purpose of Marriage Between'; subsequently only the word 'Between' is used before even it is dropped. The term 'purpose of marriage' has already been referenced in the 1698 example from Antrim. In his Foreword to the Banbridge article, Rev. W. T. Latimer, a respected historian of Presbyterianism, wrote:

> A 'purpose of marriage' was nothing more or less than a proclamation of banns, and as almost all who were proclaimed were soon afterwards married, I believe there was no separate book for registration of marriages. This opinion is supported by the fact that when marriages without proclamation were entered, this fact was recorded, and that in some of the entries the date of the marriage was entered as well as the date of the proclamation.

Latimer further noted that in recording the proclamation of the marriage the minister was proving that the rules were being followed:

> This, I think, was probably the reason why in some congregations the 'proclamation' and not the ceremony of marriage was recorded. A record of the marriage itself would not have been considered sufficient evidence by a 'Visitation Presbytery' that the Synod's law regarding proclamation had been observed.

Over 300 marriages are entered in the Banbridge register of 1756–94. The information recorded was generally limited to the date of proclamation of banns and the names of the bride and groom. In a few instances the date of marriage is also included and in every case the time lapse between the two was no more than a week. Places of residence are given, but only for people living outside the bounds of the congregation; where a location is not given it may be taken that the individual or couple were from the Banbridge congregation. The names of the witnesses are recorded for some of the later marriages. Occupations are given for a handful of grooms; e.g. John Fleming who married May Baxter in 1777 was an apothecary. Some marriages between 1784 and 1794 are stated to have taken place 'without proclamation', in which case the date is that of the marriage ceremony.

At the same Synod of 1819 that exhorted ministers to keep registers of baptisms, similar directions were given for the keeping of marriage registers:

> That every Minister of this Synod shall keep, or cause to be kept, a regular registry of all marriages celebrated by him; stating the date of each marriage, the names of the parties, the Congregations or Parishes in which they reside, and the names of at least two of the witnesses present at the celebration of the ceremony.[17]

It was also agreed that every minister would be required to submit annually to his respective presbytery an accurate list of the marriages he had conducted in the previous year. These marriages would then be copied by the Clerk of Presbytery into a separate volume. Relatively few of these presbytery marriage books seem to have survived pre-civil registration, or at least are in the public domain. One that does relates to the Tyrone Presbytery and covers marriages in the following congregations:

> Cookstown (First), 1820–8, Loughgall, 1819–22, Tobermore, 1819–22, Vinecash, 1825–8, Carland, 1826–8, Magherafelt, 1819–28, Dungannon (First), 1819–28, Benburb, 1827–8, Cloveneden, 1826–8, Richhill, 1826–8, Stewartstown (First), 1820–7, Coagh, 1820–2 and Minterburn, 1819–22 (MIC/1P/460).

It is worth noting that some of the marriage registers from this period include the names of the mother of each party, including sometimes her maiden name. Other interesting details can be recorded. The entry in the Westport register for the marriage of Fanny Grimes and Edward Evans in 1827 recorded that the bride was the grand-daughter of 'old Jas Blain, Nappah', providing us with valuable additional information on the family (PHSI).

From 1 April 1845, with the introduction of civil registration of non-Catholic marriages, the information recorded in marriage registers became standardised. The details include the name, age, status, and occupation of the persons marrying. The names and occupations of their fathers are also given. The church, the officiating minister and the witnesses to the ceremony are identified. In most cases the exact age of the parties is not given, and the entry will simply read 'full age' (i.e. over 21) or 'minor'. If the father of one of the parties was dead, this may sometimes be indicated in the marriage register by the word 'deceased' or by leaving the space blank.

On rare occasions an explanatory note was added. An example is the marriage record of the prominent trade unionist Alexander Bowman, baptised a Catholic, but raised a Presbyterian. On 30 August 1880 Bowman married Rose Ritchie in Eglinton Street Presbyterian Church, Belfast. The name of his father was entered on the marriage certificate as William McKeown. The officiating minister, Rev. Lamont Hutchinson, must have thought that this required an explanation and so drafted the following note:

> His mother was married first to a man called Bowman to whom she had a number of children. After his death she married McKeown to whom she had Alexander and some other children. He also died when his children were very young. These children began to be called by people Bowman, but without any wish on the part of their mother that it should be so. It went on nevertheless and soon their own name was lost and so it remains lost.

Occasionally records concerning the marriage of minors can be found among Presbyterian records. First Portglenone has a separate listing of marriage declarations in cases of a minor, 1886–1918 (MIC1P/24). These take the form of a signed statement by the bridegroom that he had obtained the permission of the parent(s) or guardian of the bride for the marriage to take place.

There were occasions in which the church courts of Presbyterianism acknowledged formally that a marriage had ended. In 1840–41 the Presbytery of Down deliberated over an issue that had been brought to it by the Session of the congregation of Drumlee: 'Whether a man was at liberty to marry, whose wife had deserted him, had emigrated to America, and as was believed, had been married to another man'. The Clerk of Presbytery was asked to investigate whether there was a precedent for this and eventually it was agreed that the man was 'at liberty to marry, his wife having voluntarily and without cause deserted him.'[18]

Notes

[1] Quoted in McCartney, *Carrickfergus*, p. 172.

[2] *Ordnance Survey Memoirs of Ireland Vol. 29: Parishes of County Antrim XI: Antrim Town and Ballyclare* (1995), p. 113.

[3] McCaughan, *Dunboe*, p. 69.

[4] Kilpatrick, *Millisle*, p. 28.

[5] Williamson, *May Street … Belfast*, p. 105.

[6] Blair, *Drumreagh*, pp 39–40.

[7] McFarland, *Maghera*, p. 79.

[8] Kilpatrick, *Millisle*, pp 27–8.

[9] Bonar, *Carnmoney*, p. 52.

[10] Transcribed in Gordon, *First Presbyterian Church in Belfast*, pp 58–63.

[11] *RGSU*, vol. 3, pp 511–12.

[12] Bonar, *Carnmoney*, p. 47.

[13] *Northern Whig*, 12 March 1842.

[14] A copy is in PRONI (T2957/1).

[15] For more on this subject in general, see Brian McClintock, 'The 1844 Marriage Act: politico-religious agitation and its consequence for Ulster genealogy', *Familia: Ulster Genealogical Review*, vol. 2 (1986), pp 33–58.

[16] Richard Linn and W. T. Latimer, 'Marriage register of the Presbyterian congregation of Banbridge, County Down, 1756–1794', *Journal of the Royal Society of Antiquaries of Ireland*, 5th series, vol. 39 (1909), pp 75–84.

[17] *RGSU*, vol. 3, p. 512

[18] Truesdale, *Drumlee*, p. 11.

5

Other congregational records

... a small volume, six inches by four, bound in black leather. As a result of damp and the lapse of time, several leaves at the beginning and at the end are greatly decayed. The entries extend from 1678 till 1713, and are in various handwritings; but almost all are easy to be deciphered by anyone accustomed to the style of writing which prevailed at that period.

Description of the old Session book of Dundonald[1]

5.1 Minutes of Session meetings

The Session – often called the Kirk Session – was the ruling body in a congregation and was composed of the minister and elders. The elders were chosen from among the members of the congregation, usually by a process of election, though nomination and co-option were also used. The number of elders was usually dependent on the size of the congregation and each elder was generally assigned a geographical district and made responsible for the spiritual oversight of the families living in it. One of the elders, or sometimes the minister, served as the 'Clerk of Session' and was responsible for recording the minutes of the meetings. The level of detail contained in the minutes varies between congregations and over time – sometimes the minutes can be very full, though on other occasions they can be limited in content. The minutes will usually be found in a bound volume, which may have been used exclusively for that purpose or which might also contain other congregational records.[2]

The *Guide to Church Records* lists over 200 sets of Session minutes that are accessible in PRONI, usually on microfilm, though original minute books are available in some cases. The *Guide* identifies some

Session minute books in the Presbyterian Historical Society; a fuller listing is found in the inventories of congregational records prepared by PHSI (see Chapter 3.4). Many other Session minute books remain in local custody and have never been copied and made available in an archive. The absence of minutes of Session meetings may be for the reasons outlined in Chapter 3 – destruction, neglect, etc. However, in some congregations the Session fell into abeyance for a period of time or ceased to be an effective ruling body. A presbytery visitation of Drumbo in 1845 found that there were only four ordained elders and no Session book. Eleven years later a further visitation of the congregation discovered that there was only one elder and he was irregular in his church attendance; there were no regular meetings of Session, except for those dealing with disciplinary matters, and there was still no Session book.[3]

The earliest surviving Session book is that of the congregation of Templepatrick, which was analysed and partially transcribed by Rev. W. T. Latimer upwards of a century ago.[4] The Session book begins in 1646 and continues, with some interruptions, for nearly a century, terminating in 1744. The first entry is a record of the ordination of Rev. Anthony Kennedy on the penultimate day of October 1646. In the following month a Session was formed and the names of the 14 elders are given, as well as those of four deacons. The congregation was divided into districts, to each of which an elder was assigned. The Session dealt with a range of matters within the congregation with the disciplining of errant members a major concern. For example, deliberate absence from public worship was a disciplinary matter. In 1647 the Session heard that Lieutenant Wallace 'hath some Irishes under him who comes not to the church'. Wallace was ordered to 'put them away from him or else cause them to keep the church'.

Adultery, the conception or birth of children out of wedlock, slander, unnecessary work on the Sabbath, and the use of superstitious charms were other matters that the Session dealt with. The punishments handed down included the issuing of fines and making transgressors stand before the congregation until the Session was satisfied that they had truly repented. The Templepatrick Session often deliberated on matters that in other circumstances might have been dealt with in a secular court. Baptisms were not recorded systematically in the Templepatrick Session book, but occasionally baptisms are mentioned incidentally. However, proclamations of marriage banns recur frequently. The Session book also includes accounts, showing how money was spent on providing bread and wine for Communion services and also on the support of the poor and needy.

The Aghadowey Session book of 1702–61 reveals that a similar range of matters came within its purview. The original book is in the Presbyterian Historical Society and a digital version of it can be viewed in PRONI (CR3/80).[5] For example, in 1705 the Session dealt with a dispute among some of the tenant farmers in the congregation over the occupation of certain lands. Several times the Session dealt with individuals using superstitious charms for one reason or another. In 1703 Thomas Gray came before the Session to assert that he had been falsely accused of theft by Martha Cockran and her son Andrew who had 'used that charm of turning key' in making their claims against him.[6] Martha Cockran denied the claims and Gray could provide no evidence that she had behaved in the way alleged. However, Martha did admit that her son Andrew, described as 'a child', was guilty, though he had believed there was 'no harm in it'. The Session book also includes accounts showing the distribution of funds to those in need.

Interestingly, between 1703 and 1728 more than a dozen couples were rebuked by the Aghadowey Session for having been married by a priest. For example, in 1717 Andrew Gray married Anne Thompson without the knowledge of her father Robert with the ceremony performed by 'one McGradh a popish priest'. In his history of Aghadowey, Rev. T. H. Mullin surmises that rather than being examples of mixed marriages, the reason that these marriages were conducted by priests was the absence of parental consent.[7] The same issue crops up in other Session books. For example, on 8 August 1765 Andrew Davison and Elizabeth Grant appeared before the Session of First Dromara Presbyterian Church 'confessing their sin and offence of irregular marriage by a popish priest'; they were rebuked before the Session and again publicly before the congregation (MIC1P/89/2).

Due to its dissent from the political status quo, the Reformed Presbyterian Church considered a number of actions to be disciplinary matters which were not regarded as such by other denominations. In particular, the Church objected to voting in parliamentary elections. Many members, however, did vote and in the wake of elections the minutes of Session meetings in Reformed

Presbyterian congregations frequently included the censuring of members for having voted. The earliest surviving Session minutes of what was known as the Antrim Congregation (combining Cullybackey and Kellswater), covering the years 1789–1802, include several references to individuals being censured for voting or taking part in elections (CR5/5/9A/1). In 1790 John Atchinson appeared before Session and confessed that he had voted in the most recent election; he was reprimanded for having done so. In the same year John Kerns was rebuked by Session for appearing at Carrickfergus during an election and for wearing party colours, though he denied that he had actually voted. The Reformed Presbyterian Church was also opposed to members joining the Orange Order and Freemasons and disciplined individuals who enlisted in these organisations.

Occasionally more unusual items will be found in Session books. The following declaration of 1826 is found in the First Dunboe Session book and was signed by 50 members of the congregation:

> We the minister, elders, and members of the Presbyterian congregation of Dunboe, having long contemplated with regret the pernicious consequences of the use of spirituous liquors at wakes and funerals, and anxious to put a stop to a practice so destructive of the morals of the people and so injurious to the growth of true and vital religion, do hereby resolve: that from this day forward, we will not allow in any house or family over which we have authority, the public distribution of spirituous liquors upon such occasions; that we will not partake of them where they are so distributed; and that we will use the whole of our influence to prevent others from partaking, out of concern for their temporal and spiritual welfare.[8]

Tributes to deceased members, usually elders, can also be included in Session minutes, though these tend to focus on the character and qualities of the deceased rather than his life and family. The following minute was added to the Session book of Bready Reformed Presbyterian Church following the passing of James McIntosh, an elder in the congregation, in 1899:

> Our brother occupied a large place in the history of our congregation. During a period of 40 years, Mr McIntosh faithfully discharged the duties of ruling elder. Possessed of a strong mind, unwearied and self-sacrificing in the performance of duty, his brother elders looked up to

him with confidence as a leader and guide. As treasurer of the congregation for a long series of years, he discharged the difficult duties devolving on him with the utmost diligence.[9]

5.2 Minutes of committee meetings

In the early days of organised Presbyterianism in Ireland the role of the Session extended beyond the spiritual oversight of the congregation. In time, however, most congregations formed committees or, less often, elected and ordained deacons[10] to take charge of such matters as the maintenance of the meeting house, and the collection and disbursing of church funds, including payments to the minister and others, such as the precentor and sexton, as well as the distribution of money for the poor. Minutes of the meetings of these committees were usually kept and in many instances these can also be accessed in public archives, including PRONI and the Presbyterian Historical Society.

A few congregations formed committees in the eighteenth century. In 1760 a committee was formed (or re-elected?) in the First Presbyterian Church in Belfast and it was agreed that 'a book be kept in the Session-house wherein the transactions of the Committee shall be regularly entered and the minutes of every meeting signed by the Chairman'.[11] In 1778 rules to be followed by the committee of Millisle Presbyterian Church were prepared. In summary these were: 1) meetings would be held on the second Sunday of each month either before the sermon or at the interval in the service; 2) meetings would be presided over by the committee members in rotation based on age; 3) decisions would be made by majority voting; 4) the committee would not interfere in the work of the Session; and 5) a collection would be lifted at the doors of the meeting house on the first Sunday of each month.[12]

The creation of a congregational committee could be in response to a specific set of circumstances. For instance, the formation of a committee in Bready Reformed Presbyterian Church in 1806 was for better managing the temporal affairs of 'the house being new modelled', suggesting that the congregation's place of worship was undergoing renovations. The membership of the committee was representative of the congregation at large for each 'society' (see Chapter 1 for the society system in the RP Church) nominated individuals to sit on it. Committee members were to take their duties seriously. Latecomers would be fined five pence, while those who failed to turn up at all would be fined 15 pence – this would be doubled for a second offence.[13]

5.3 Calls to ministers

When the members of a Presbyterian congregation identified a man they wanted to be their minister they issued what was known as a 'call'. This was a written invitation to him which set out the reasons for the call and which was signed by the members of the congregation. It was then up to the individual to whom the call was issued to decide whether or not to accept the call. Some of these calls include fairly extensive lists of names. For example, the call issued to Thomas Clark by the Seceders of County Monaghan in 1751 contains the names of over 160 individuals.[14] A call to John Cameron by the members of Dunluce in 1755 runs to a comparable total.[15] A most interesting call is the one that was issued in 1772 to Rev. William Stavely by the 'Covenanted electors between the Bridge of Dromore and Donaghadee in the County of Down', which was signed by over 90 individuals; a copy of this call is in the Historical Library of the Reformed Theological College, Knockbracken.

By way of example, the following is the wording of the call to Rev. J. W. Calderwood from the congregation of Bready on 2 June 1924:

> We, the Office-bearers and members of the Reformed Presbyterian congregation of Bready under the inspection of the Western Presbytery, being without a fixed pastor, and being well assured by good information and our own experience of the piety, prudence, learning, soundness in the faith, and attachment to the Testimony of the Church, as also to the suitableness to our capacities of you Mr Jas W. Calderwood have agreed with the concurrence of Presbytery aforesaid, to call you; and we hereby do heartily invite, call and entreat you to undertake the office of pastor among us. Upon your accepting of this our Call, and discharging ministerial duties among us, we promise you all dutiful respect, obedience, encouragement, and support in the Lord.[16]

The call was witnessed by two individuals who were not members of the congregation, but lived near the meeting house, and signed by the elders first and then by the members. Mr Calderwood accepted the call and remained minister of Bready until his death in 1971.

Calls to ministers can be found among the records of the congregation and some are listed in the PRONI *Guide to Church Records*. Others may be found by searching PRONI's online eCatalogue. The records held by the Presbyterian Historical Society include a number of calls to ministers. The Ulster Museum has copies of several calls made out to ministers named Kennedy:

> Call to Rev. George Kennedy to Lisburn, 11 Dec. 1774; call to Rev.
> Gilbert Kennedy to Killyleagh, 27 Dec. 1732 – Acc. 604, 605–1914
> Call to Rev. Gilbert Kennedy to the New Congregation of Protestant
> Dissenters in Belfast (i.e. Second Belfast), 7 March 1744 – Acc.
> 606–1914
> Call to Rev. Andrew Kennedy to Mourne, 18 Jan. 1740 [1741];
> declaration of the congregation of Mourne promising to pay Kennedy
> for his pastoral services, 24 Feb. 1740 [1741] – Acc. 607, 608–1914

Some calls remain in the possession of the descendants of the minister. Others can turn up in the most unusual of places. For example, among the papers of the Hely-Hutchinson family, earls of Donoughmore, which were at the family seat at Knocklofty, County Tipperary, is the original of the call to James Bond to become pastor of the congregation of Corboy, County Longford. Dated 17 January 1722 [1723] and drawn up at the meeting-house of Corboy, the signatories to the call asked Bond 'to take the charge and oversight of us in the Lord, earnestly beseeching you to embrace this our call as from God'. A photocopy of the call is in PRONI (T3459/B/5/1). A grand-daughter of James Bond married a Hely-Hutchinson and this may explain the presence of the document among the papers of that family.[17]

5.4 Visiting books, communicants' lists, etc

Documents detailing the members and families connected with a congregation are a real boon to any researcher. These can come in different forms. At their simplest they may be no more than a list of names. More detailed items may provide the townland and the names of all members of the family, along with annotations providing additional details, such as when someone married, died or emigrated. The *Guide to Church Records* will indicate if such records are available in PRONI (often they are described in the *Guide* simply as 'census'), while for records in the Presbyterian Historical Society see the PHSI listings of congregational records. Congregational histories often reproduce these listings of names and some of them have made their way into local history books and journals. An example of the latter is Theo McMahon and Maire O Neill, 'Census of First Monaghan Presbyterian Congregation, 1821', *Clogher Record*, vol. 19 (2006), pp 94–110.

The creation of a record of the families in a congregation was often to assist the minister in his work of pastoral visitation. In 1822, the recently ordained minister of Convoy in County Donegal, Rev. John Wray, prepared a register of the 184 families in his congregation. Arranged by townland, this records the names of each member of the household, as well as the maiden names of married women and the ages of many of the children. Mullin reproduced the names in his history of Convoy, along with Wray's additional comments such as 'Extinct', 'America' and 'Australia', though perhaps understandably without including the 'occasionally pungent comments on the religious condition of the family'.[18]

Visitation records kept by Rev. Samuel Hamilton of Buckna exist for the period 1849–70 and were reproduced in facsimile in Margaret Millar's history of the congregation (the originals were in private possession). These records are arranged by townland and give the name of the head of each household with further details such as the number of children, and occasionally additional family relationships and occupation. Added comments include 'husband to America', 'non compos mentis', 'wife from Gracehill', 'keep little shop', 'deaf as door nail' and '24 years old & has only heard three sermons'.[19] The records of the former Presbyterian congregation of Carrigallen, County Leitrim, include a visitation book with details of each family by townland and dates of baptisms of children, 1837–92 (MIC1P/163). The notebook kept by the minister of Banagher, Rev. William James Dalrymple Williamson, recording details of visits to members of the congregation in the late 1800s, includes information on the church attendance and health, among other things, of the members (MIC1P/456/1). At the back of the volume there is a record of funeral addresses.

Some ministers went into incredible detail on the families in their congregation. The following is an excerpt from 'Some Statisticks of

The Families of the Congregation of Ballygilbert by The Pastor, the Rev. Abraham Liggat January 1846':

> Adair, James. His father Wm died in B[ally]sallagh. His mother's maiden name Jane Henderson – her father Laird Henderson, both dead – she died about 30 years ago – James's father Wm died about six years ago. The family according to age were Sarah, married, lives near Killinchy; Wm, bachelor, lives in B.sallagh, was imprisoned 9 months for theft in B[ally]leidy, is about 50 years of age; Mary Ann married to Jno. Mewha embarked a considerable time ago for America; Margt married to Henry Claney, farmer, lives at Orlock near Donagha[dee]; Sophia married to Geo. Patterson, farmer, near Bangor ... (T2643/1)

A truly remarkable volume is Rev. Robert Magill's family record book for the congregation of First Antrim (Millrow): 'Names of seat-holders and their families and also names etc. of such individuals as belong to the congregation but have no seat. Extracted from the records of the parish and other documents by the Revd. Robert Magill.' This includes detailed information on the families that belonged to the congregation in the early nineteenth century, including baptisms, marriages, deaths and places of burial. On a number of occasions Magill even went so far as to sketch out family trees, with figure drawings of the various family members. His volume is available for inspection at the Presbyterian Historical Society. Less common is a document along the lines of the following item of 1854 deriving from the records of Portaferry: 'List of persons nominally presbyterian but whose names are not in the ... List of Portaferry congregation' (D2709/2/6).

An important role of the Session was the admittance of individuals, having given satisfactory answers to the questions put to them, to full communicant membership in the congregation and the regulation of the sacrament of the 'Lord's Supper'. The names of those admitted to membership can be found in Session minutes. In addition, there may be a roll listing the communicant members of a congregation (i.e. those who, having been admitted to membership by the Session, were allowed to take part in Communion services). Sometimes there may be a separate list of the names of new communicants. Occasionally lists of communicants are annotated with additional information, such as when a communicant married, emigrated or died. Notes on emigration can be helpful in following the movements of former members of a congregation. For example the communicants' roll of Middletown Presbyterian Church records that William Vogan of Feduff had moved to Belfast by December 1877 and had emigrated to Canada by 1889 (MIC1P/212).

A roll of communicants for Second Stewartstown[20] drawn up in 1871 includes details on those who were struck off for various reasons including: gone to America; absent for years, no cause assigned save poverty; residing near Dublin; and joined Methodists. Other names were kept on the roll, but were given various admonitions. One lady was unable to walk, but her husband was urged to 'bring her out in a convenience'. Another couple had been members previously of the nearby congregation of Brigh, but due to a 'quarrel', had left without obtaining certificates and had not been at Communion since. A further couple had absented themselves due to a row with another family over a seat. No doubt some of these issues vexed the Session more than others as they tried to be consistent in their approach.

Other records giving the names of members of a congregation include poll lists drawn up in advance of an election of a new minister. An example is the poll list drawn up in the congregation of Aghadowey following the death of the minister in 1874. It names those eligible to vote; if the person sat in the gallery this is indicated and in some instances the townland of residence is given. A transcription of this list is available on the PHSI website (members only). A copy of another such list is available in PRONI for Draperstown Presbyterian Church from 1886 (T3232/7).

Occasionally there may be a list of names within the records of a congregation that does not fall easily into any particular category. It may have been produced in response to certain issues affecting the congregation. For example, within the communicants' roll book for Dundalk Presbyterian Church are a number of loose pages. One set of these pages is titled 'In re-Memorial for Instrumental Aid' and dated 1 July 1901. It contains 238 names in favour and 11 names of people who were not opposed, but who would not sign (Louth County Archives, PP00075/001/003). In the 1870s there was a row in Ballyalbany Presbyterian Church over an item of apparel worn by the minister. Following the ordination of James Bodel as minister of this congregation in 1873, some of the women presented him with a pulpit gown. However, many members objected to Bodel's wearing of this with some threatening to leave the congregation on account of it. The gown was stolen, but later handed in. Those who objected to the gown drew up a memorial, signed by five elders and 117 communicants (and including townland addresses), which was presented to the minister.[21]

For some Reformed Presbyterian congregations there are copies of the documents drafted in the 1850s when 'Covenant Renewal' (the reaffirmation of the Covenants of 1638 and 1643) was being encouraged. PRONI holds two items concerning 'Covenant Renewal' in Kilraughts Reformed Presbyterian Church in 1855, which are signed by the elders and others (CR5/15/1A–B). Other 'Covenant Renewal' documents remain in local custody. The 'Draught of an Act of Covenant Renovation' prepared by the congregation of Ballylaggan in May 1856 is copied into the Session minute book along with 128 names of those giving their assent to it. The relevant pages have been reproduced in facsimile in a history of the congregation.[22] Since no registers of this congregation are in the public domain, this is a hugely important source of information on the membership in the mid nineteenth century.[23]

5.5 Migration records and transfer certificates

As already highlighted, details concerning the arrival and departure of families and individuals can be found in many congregational records. For instance, a list of members of Clough Non-Subscribing Presbyterian Church includes the following details for the Hagan family of Drumnaquoile: 'Robert and Samuel Hagan, sons of Robert Hagan, Drumnaquoile, by the first wife, sailed from Glasgow in the Stormcloud for New Zealand on the 1st May 1864' (CR4/16/D/1). On occasion there may be documents that specifically relate to the departure of families and individuals from a congregation. PRONI has a list of members of the Portaferry congregation who left to live in other parts of Ireland or who emigrated to Australia, America, New Zealand or England, 1852–72 (D2709/2/4). Likewise for Gortin there are lists of emigrants, 1854–84 (MIC1P/253/1).

A member of one congregation who wished to move to another could apply to the Session for a transfer certificate testifying to his or her good standing in the church. This was a handwritten document, signed by the minister and at least some of the elders. They are also known as testimonials and certificates of disjunction. Within Ireland these were often issued to women moving to another congregation on marriage or a family that was relocating due to new work opportunities. The records of Carnmoney Presbyterian Church include the names of those who transferred from other congregations during the period 1708–25. Appendix 3 of Robert Bonar's history of this congregation has a breakdown of the originating congregations of these 400+ testimonials.[24] Not surprisingly, most of the new members came from local congregations, notably Ballyclare, Ballyeaston and Templepatrick. Others came from much further afield, including Carlingford in County Louth, Letterkenny in County Donegal and Dublin. In addition, 11 men, 11 women and four families brought testimonials from Scotland in these years.

Another very early set of testimonials survives for Ballynahinch and covers the period 1715–34 (CR3/69).[25] Like the Carnmoney testimonials these also reveal that most people seeking admittance to Ballynahinch came from local congregations. Here too there are also records of people from Scotland and though only a small sample, these are revealing of their places of origin.

1715	Heaktor McNeall, testimonial from Scotland dated 18 March 1710 subscribed by Mr Daniell McClavrin [possibly Daniel Maclaurin, minister of Kilfinan, Argyll]
1716	Sarah Cloaky, testimonial from Whithorn, Scotland subscribed by Mr John McCaull
1717	Margaret Cherry, testimonial from Midcader [Mid Calder] in Scotland dated 1711 subscribed by Moses Cherry
1725	Robert Gordon, testimonial from Portpatrick
1725	Agnes Clokey testimonial from Whithorn
1729–31	Margaret Foster produced one from Scotland by Mr John Hunter [possibly the minister of Ayr]
1729–31[?]	Makready produced one from Stranraer by Mr Laired
1732	Samuel Mack and his wife, testimonial from Scotland subscribed by Mr William Cupples [possibly the minister of Kirkoswald, Ayrshire]

Transfer certificates were also issued to those who were preparing to emigrate to another part of the world. One of the earliest to survive is the certificate granted to William and Margaret Bryan by the Session of the congregation of Ballyroney on 17 April 1718.[26] The certificate is in private possession in America, but a photograph of it is on display in Ballyroney Presbyterian Church. The document notes that William Bryan, 'a useful Member of this Congregation', was 'now about to transport himself and his family to America'. William and his wife Margaret were described as 'of good repute amongst us' and 'of a blameless and Gospel Conversation'. The certificate was signed by the minister, Rev. James Moor, and 11 others who believed that the Bryans 'so Deserve Encouragement & a kind and cheerful reception into any christian Society where the Providence of God may cast their lot'. The Bryans moved to Pennsylvania before relocating to New Jersey and later settling in Virginia.

In some congregations there were efforts to formalise the procedure for granting a disjunction certificate. The Session of Millisle ruled in 1820 that 'all certificates granted to persons leaving the congregation or removing from the country must be given at a meeting of the elders, and signed by the Minister and Session Clerk'. Furthermore, before a certificate was issued the individual had to settle any outstanding debts to the congregation, unless poverty prevented him from doing so. Sometimes there will be a separate listing of certificates granted. The records of Second Dunboe include a listing of certificates received and certificates granted (usually including the intended destination of the person or persons to whom the certificate was issued) for the years 1841–7 (MIC/1P/149A–D).

5.6 Financial records

Documentation relating to church finances survives in different forms. Details of income and expenditure can be found in Session and committee minute books, as can the names of contributors to church funds. On other occasions there may be separate account books and stipend lists; likewise there can be separate books for pew rents or they might be found within other congregational volumes. Good examples of account books are those kept by the Presbyterian congregation in Princes Street, Cork (now the Unitarian Church), which cover the years 1758–1822 (Cork City and County Archives, U025). These provide a fascinating insight into the workings of the congregation during an important period in its history. The descriptive list (available as a downloadable PDF from the archive's website) includes a list of the names appearing in the account books, giving the years in which the individual first and last appears.

Congregational funds derived from two principal sources, the more important of which by far was the income from pew rents, i.e. the monies generated by the letting of pews or seats within the meeting house. Chapter 8 looks in more detail at seating arrangements in meeting houses and the records relating to the collection of pew rents. Prior to the early to mid twentieth century pew rents provided the greater part of the minister's stipend (salary) contributed by his congregation. As the following declaration in the First Ballybay records indicates, each stipend-payer made a binding commitment to pay a specific amount of money on certain dates during the year:

> We whose names are underwritten, members of the Presbyterian congregation of Ballibay, do promise to pay to the collectors for the time being, the several sums annexed to our names, for the support of said congregation, in four equal shares, or quarterly payments, the first payment to be made on the first day of August next, and on the fast day of every succeeding quarter as long as we remain members of said congregation Given under our hands 24th day of May, 1818.[27]

The fulfilment of these commitments was of great importance in providing financial stability to a congregation. A stipend list of Carlingford Presbyterian Church begins 'with the names of those on whose promised aid the Congregation was at first organized by the authority of the General Assembly 1868' and runs annually until 1903 (Louth County Archives, PP00075/001/005). In the course of the twentieth century congregations replaced the payment of pew rents/stipend with 'freewill offerings' – contributions made on a weekly, monthly or less regular basis in sealed envelopes.

In addition to the income from pew rents there were also weekly collections. The money raised in this way was applied to a variety of uses. A very early set of accounts is available for Ballynahinch: 'An Account of what Collections & Disbursments hath been in this Congregation since M[r]. Hendry Livingston become our Minister', 1704–34 (CR3/69).[28] These accounts reveal the ways in which the congregation spent money on providing bread and wine for Communion services, on covering the expenses of the elder delegated to attend meetings on behalf of the Session, and on the maintenance of the meeting house. Most of the names appearing in these accounts are of the poor who were supported by the congregation; the same names recur frequently. Occasionally people from further afield also received assistance, such as in 1718 when James Thompson of Comber was given five shillings after his house burned down. Other names include tradesmen and craftsmen who carried out work to the church and those who borrowed the congregation's mort-cloth for funerals.

Provision for the poor continued well into the nineteenth century and in some congregations into the twentieth century. In Kilraughts the 'Poor Money', which was not necessarily restricted to members of the congregation, was distributed by the Session at the start of each year to those in most need. Some of the payments made in the years 1816–18 include the costs of making coffins and burying the poor. For example, in 1817 Weeda Bredy was paid £0 4s. 8d. for the burial of her mother, while in 1818 the payment of five shillings was made for Jean Smiley's coffin.[29] The records of Dundalk Presbyterian Church include 'An account of the collection and distribution of poor's money in the Presbyterian Congregation of Dundalk', 1831–9 (Louth County Archives, PP00075/001/001). A Widows and Orphans Society was established by Limerick Presbyterian Church and its surviving committee book, 1856–71, and account book, 1856–89, are in PHSI. Carnmoney Presbyterian Church had a printed application form to be completed on behalf of those requiring assistance from the congregation. This provided details on the applicant, including name, age, health and attendance at Communion and public worship. An example is reproduced in Robert Bonar's history of Carnmoney.[30]

From around the mid 1800s printed financial statements or reports began to be issued, both by individual congregations and by presbyteries. Often these will simply be a list of contributors (sometimes identified as stipend-payers or seatholders) and the amount paid by each. Occasionally places of residence are included. By the late 1800s the financial offerings were often broken down into stipend or pew rent, Sustentation Fund and sometimes even contributions towards missions. PRONI has printed financial reports for a number of congregations and presbyteries and many of those produced by congregations are listed in the *Guide to Church Records*. With regard to financial reports issued at presbytery level, PRONI has the following items:

Armagh Presbytery, 1881, 1882, 1892 – D1814/10, /11A, /12
Derry Presbytery, 1876, 1880, 1888, 1890–91 – CR3/46/4/2/A/1–4
Dromore Presbytery, 1924 – CR3/35/2
Limavady Presbytery, 1909–26 – D1090/5/1
Strabane Presbytery, 1936–56 – D1386/20

For the Ballymena area, see *Listing Mid-Antrim Presbyterians in 1864: Annual Reports of the Congregations in Connexion with the Ballymena Presbytery for the Year Ending May, 1864*, published by the Mid-Antrim Historical Group in 1996. The Linen Hall Library in Belfast has financial reports for several presbyteries, including Carrickfergus (1923), Down (1883–4), Dungannon (1877, 1890, 1895, 1901–04, 1907–21, 1923–25), Letterkenny (1865), Strabane (1861–1952), and Omagh (1868, 1883). Further financial reports are in PHSI. Congregational histories often reproduce financial reports for selected years, frequently in facsimile.

5.7 Other congregational records

Within each congregation there could be a number of organisations, ranging from the purely recreational to bodies established to promote an interest in missionary endeavour. In Sandymount Presbyterian Church, Dublin, there was a Literary and Social Union, the minutes of which for 1866–80 are in PHSI. Surviving records of organisations catering for youth include the Young People's Guild committee minutes, 1901–03, and report, 1904–5 for First Newry, Sandy's Street (PHSI). Minutes of the Juvenile Missionary Association, 1926–67, are available for the former Chancellor Memorial Reformed Presbyterian Church in Belfast (CR5/2/2/5/5). PRONI has a minute book for the years 1909–16 of Fisherwick Women's Working Association, Belfast, an organisation that, among other things, encouraged an interest in and support for missions (D1812/1). The records of Dunmurry Presbyterian Church include minutes of the Women's Association for Foreign Missions, 1930–8 and 1955–62 (MIC1P/453/6).

Other organisations were designed to promote temperance or even total abstinence from alcohol. The records of Banagher Presbyterian Church include a membership register of the Banagher Temperance Association, 1857–1900 (MIC1P/227), while those for Portrush Presbyterian Church include a register of members of the Portrush Total Abstinence Society, 1845–94 (MIC1P/415). For Newtownards Reformed Presbyterian Church there is a pledge book of the Total Abstinence Association, 1869–1906 (CR/5/11). Found among the papers of Rev. William Kennedy McKay of First Portglenone is a list of the names of subscribers to the Portglenone Temperance Society in 1831 (D2594/4D). The Band of Hope, a temperance organisation which was co-founded by Ann Jane Carlile,[31] the widow of a Presbyterian minister in Bailieborough, was established in a number of congregations. Available records include a list of members of Killeter Band of Hope in 1857 (PHSI, CR29) and the membership register of the Band of Hope in Ekenhead, Belfast, 1874–96 (MIC1P/8). Between 1881 and 1885 a charitable association called the Dorcas Society operated within Cuningham Memorial Presbyterian Church in Cullybackey, which provided clothing and other fabric items, such as blankets and handkerchiefs, to those in need.[32]

Printed annual reports are available for some congregations from the second half of the nineteenth century onwards. These may include reports from the different bodies within the congregation, such as the Session, committee and Sunday school. Taking the Reformed Presbyterian Church in College Street South, Belfast, as an example, the printed *Annual Reports* for the year ending 31 October 1874 includes an 'Introductory Address & Review by Session', followed by reports from the Deacons (including the Stipend List, naming contributors to the stipend and the value of their financial offering), the Juvenile Missionary Association (with the names of collectors to the Association's funds and how much each had collected), the Sabbath School (naming the teachers), and the Temperance Association. Finally, there is a list of names and addresses of the members of the congregation, arranged by 'society' (e.g. Ballymacarett Society, Falls Road Society).

Defying easy categorisation is a remarkable document from 1875 which has been titled the Dublin Presbyterian Colporteur's Notebook. In 1874 Ormond Quay Presbyterian Church in Dublin advertised for a colporteur with the successful candidate, William B. Malone, assuming his position on the first day of 1875. While the work of a colporteur is generally the distribution of religious tracts, the role of the Ormond Quay colporteur was more that of a missionary. Malone's job specification included the stipulation that he was to spend at least five hours each working day 'seeking out and visiting unconnected Presbyterian families first, then Protestants of any denomination not attached to any place of worship'. He was directed to keep a record of all 'unconnected families' in the Ormond Quay district (though his work extended through a wider area of inner-city Dublin). Following his instructions carefully, Malone produced a detailed record of more than 10,000 Protestants of different denominations. In addition to listing names and addresses, Malone also recorded personal observations on those with whom he came into contact. The notebook has been scanned by the Irish Genealogical Research Society and made available online for members of the Society (www.irishancestors.ie).

Notes

[1] W. T. Latimer, 'The old session book of the Presbyterian congregation at Dundonald', *UJA*, 2nd series, vol. 3 (July 1893), p. 227.

[2] For example, the Session minutes for First Antrim for the years 1842–54 are found in a volume that also contains: accounts, 1840–61; baptisms, 1839–40; accounts for money received for baptisms and marriages 1842–52; and a register of certificates given to members leaving, 1842–50 (CR3/2/A/2).

[3] Reid, *Drumbo*, p. 48

[4] W. T. Latimer, 'The old session-book of Templepatrick Presbyterian Church', *JRSAI*, 5th series, vol. 5 (1895), pp 130–34; vol. 11 (1901), pp 162–75, 259–72.

[5] Following the death of the Rev. Dr John Brown of Aghadowey in 1873, his nephew and executor, Rev. John Brown, gave the session book to the Misses Thompson of Cullycapple, Aghadowey, because of their family's long association with the congregation. Pasted on the inside of the front cover is a page from the *Irish Presbyterian* of December 1909 which reported the donation of the session book to the Presbyterian Historical Society of Ireland.

[6] The 'turning key' was a method of divination used in England and New England at this time to find stolen items and catch thieves – see Andrew Sneddon, *Witchcraft and Magic in Ireland* (2015).

[7] Mullin, *Aghadowey*, p. 144.

[8] McCaughan, *Dunboe*, p. 71.

[9] Roulston, *Bready*, pp 134–5.

[10] Deacons were chosen by the members of the congregation and ordained to office for life. There were moves to replace committees with deacons in many Reformed Presbyterian congregations in the mid nineteenth century.

[11] Moore, *First Belfast*, p. 136.

[12] Kilpatrick, *Millisle*, p. 19.

[13] Roulston, *Bready*, pp 80–81.

[14] Orr and Haslett, *Ballyalbany*, pp 10–12.

[115] Mullin, *Dunluce*, pp 83–4.

[16] Images of the call are reproduced in Roulston, *Bready*, pp 173–4.

[17] The Donoughmore papers are now in the Manuscripts & Archives Research Library of Trinity College Dublin. The PRONI eCatalogue erroneously lists the year of the call as 1772.

[18] Mullin, *Convoy*, pp 177–191.

[19] Millar, *Buckna*, pp 199–254.

[20] Reproduced in *On the Meeting House Steps … Stewartstown*, pp 83–5.

[21] Orr and Haslett, *Ballyalbany*, pp 101–06.

[22] Wright, *Ballylaggan*, pp 23–5.

[23] A Covenant signed by members of the Secession congregation of Roseyards, dated 18 July 1764, with a renewal dated 11 Oct. 1780, is in PRONI (D1748/A/2).

[24] Bonar, *Carnmoney*, pp 318–19; some examples are illustrated on page 300.

[25] Also available online at https://rosdavies.com and in the members' area of the UHF website (www.ancestryireland.com).

[26] See the article by John Lockington on 'The Bryans of Ballyroney', *BPHSI*, vol. 43 (2019), pp 56–8.

[27] Nesbitt, *Ballybay*, p. 59.

[28] Also available online at https://rosdavies.com and in the members' area of the UHF website (www.ancestryireland.com).

[29] Blair, *Kilraughts*, pp 56–7.

[30] Bonar, *Carnmoney*, p. 304.

[31] Leslie McKeague, *Anne Jane Carlile, 1775–1864, Prison Reformer and Temperance Pioneer* (2015).

[32] Megaw, *Cullybackey*, pp 145–6.

6

Records of the higher courts
and other Presbyterian bodies

6.1 Records of the higher courts

There are several layers of church government in the presbyterian system, all of which generate a range of records. The following sections initially look at the availability of records of the higher courts by denomination before discussing the value of research in the records created by them. Researchers should also be aware that reports of the meetings of presbyteries and the General Assembly and the higher courts of other Presbyterian denominations were published in the press, especially from the early 1800s onwards, and frequently a more detailed account might be reported in a newspaper than recorded in the actual minutes of the meeting.

Synod of Ulster/General Assembly

No records survive of the inaugural Irish Presbytery formed in 1642. The earliest records of an officially constituted body of Presbyterian ministers and elders in Ireland are the minutes of the 'Antrim Meeting', one of three sub-presbyteries that were established in 1654 as intermediate bodies between congregations and the Presbytery. The original minute book of the Antrim Meeting, covering the years 1654–8, is in the Gamble Library of Union Theological College. A transcription of it has been published: Mark S. Sweetnam (ed.), *The Minutes of the Antrim Ministers' Meeting 1654–8* (2012). Other early records of this nature include the minutes of the Laggan presbytery, which begin in 1672 and run to 1700 (CR/5/5E/2; D/1759/1E/1–2; MIC637/6). This presbytery was focused primarily on County Donegal, west County Tyrone and the environs of the city of Derry. The minute book was quarried extensively by Rev. A.

G. Lecky for his books, *The Laggan and its Presbyterianism* (1905) and *In the Days of the Laggan Presbytery* (1908).[1]

The most extensive collection of original and transcribed presbytery books is held by the Presbyterian Historical Society, including records dating from as far back as the second half of the seventeenth century. There are presbytery records from across Ireland including, for example, the minutes of the Dublin Presbytery, 1786–1818 (PBY 23/1/1–2). PRONI has a large number of copies and transcripts of presbytery records, many of them the work of Rev. David Stewart (D1759; MIC637). Other records in PRONI include the 'General Presbytery Book' for Dublin, 1730–39 (D2907/1). Union Theological College holds the minute books of some presbyteries, including those of the Presbytery of Belfast, 1774–1800, and the Presbytery of Derry, 1764–96. In addition to the regular meetings of the presbytery there may have been sub-committees dealing with various matters. Records generated by these bodies include the minute book of the Education Board of the Tyrone Presbytery, 1890–1965 (CR3/46/4/1/B/1). Other minutes of presbytery education boards include those of the Athlone Presbytery, 1894–1930, and the Cork Presbytery, 1893–1933, in PHSI.

The minutes of the meetings of the Synod of Ulster for the period 1691–1820 were published in three volumes in the late nineteenth century: *Records of the General Synod of Ulster* (1890–98), now available on the Internet Archive (archive.org). Minutes of the meetings of the General Synod are available in PRONI for most years in the 1830s (CR3/46/9). Sets of printed minutes of the General Assembly are in PRONI (CR3/46/2), the Presbyterian Historical Society, and other libraries. The Presbyterian Church also established a number of regional sub-synods, including the Sub-Synod of Derry; its minutes for 1706–36 and 1744–1802 are available in the Presbyterian Historical Society; PRONI holds a copy of the minutes for 1706–36 (CR3/46/3/1).

Secession Church

Transcriptions made by Rev. David Stewart of the minute books of the Burgher Synod, 1779–1818, and Antiburgher Synod, 1788–1818, are available in PRONI (D/3815/D/3–4). The main collection of Stewart's papers in PRONI (D1759; MIC637) has other transcriptions of minute books of the higher courts of the Seceders in Ireland. There is also a typescript of extracts from the minute book of the Scottish Secession Synod, 1736–82, which includes information relating to Ireland (D1759/1F/3; MIC637/7). Minutes of the united Secession Synod are available in PRONI for the years 1818–23 (CR3/46/1/2A). Other records of the presbyteries and synods of the Secession Church are available in PHSI. With regard to those Seceder congregations that remained outside of the Union of the Synods in 1840, the National Records of Scotland in Edinburgh holds the minutes of the Down and Derry Original Secession Presbytery, 1842–51 (CH3/79/1), and United Presbyterian Presbytery of Ireland, 1858–70 (CH3/181/2).

Non-Subscribing Church

Photostat copies of the 'minutes and records' of the non-subscribing Presbytery of Antrim for the years 1783–1863 are available in PRONI (T1053). PRONI also has typescript minutes of the Presbytery of Armagh of the Remonstrant Synod, 1825–32 (CR4/1/D/1–2) and a minute book of the Northern Presbytery of Antrim, 1870–95 (CR4/1/F/1), as well as 'A brief account of the formation of the Free Congregational Union, 1876-80' (CR4/1/A/16). The papers of Rev. David Stewart in PRONI include extracts from the minutes of the Remonstrant Synod, 1830–73 (D1759/1/C/1; MIC637/2). Some documents concerning the Synod of Munster can be found in the Dublin Unitarian Church Collection in the Royal Irish Academy.

Reformed Presbyterian Church

Unfortunately, there are no surviving minutes of the Reformed Presbytery prior to the early nineteenth century. PRONI has several copies of the minutes of the Reformed Presbytery for the years 1803–10 (CR5/5/A/1/2–5). In 1810 the decision was made to subdivide the Reformed Presbytery into four regional presbyteries which were to be under the authority of a Synod. PRONI has copies of the minutes of the Synod from 1811 to 1956 (CR5/5/A/1 *passim*). The printed minutes of the Synod are available in the Historical Library of the Reformed Theological College, Knockbracken. PRONI also has minutes of the Northern Presbytery (CR5/5/B/1), Eastern Presbytery (CR5/5/B/4) and Western Presbytery (MIC/1C/1/3), all beginning in 1811, though with gaps.

6.2 Using the records of the higher courts for research

Presbytery is the middle layer of government in the Presbyterian Church, above Session and below Synod and General Assembly. Each presbytery comprises those congregations located within a specified geographical area. Presbytery meetings are attended in an official capacity by the minister and a representative elder of each congregation within the presbytery. Presbytery meetings are held on a regular basis and minutes of their proceedings are recorded by the appointed clerk (usually a minister). Historically, presbyteries have had several spheres of responsibility.[2] These included the supervision, training and licensing to preach of candidates for the ministry, and the ordination and installation of pastors to congregations. Matters that could not be resolved at congregational level were brought to presbytery, as were issues that affected more than one congregation. Presbyteries conducted periodic 'visitations' of congregations, during which the spiritual and material affairs of the congregation were analysed. The 'findings' of these visitations include information on the number of elders, the times and frequency of services, the numbers of members and adherents; the condition of the meeting house; and whether or not congregational records were being kept adequately.

Presbyteries have been frequently reorganised in response to various developments, such as an increase in the number of congregations in a region or controversies associated with the issue of subscription. The growth of Presbyterianism in the west of Ireland led to the creation of the Presbytery of Connaught in 1825. In 1834, following calls for something to be done about the 'inconvenience arising in Presbyterial business from the present disproportionate division', there was a major reorganisation of the network of presbyteries in the Synod of Ulster. Taking the example of one congregation, over the course of its history Maghera has been in the following presbyteries: Antrim, 1654–7; Route, 1657–1702; Tyrone, 1702–37; Route, 1737–1834; Magherafelt, 1834–1950; Magherahoghill, 1950–61; and Tyrone, 1961–present.[3] In addition, individual congregations were sometimes transferred from one presbytery to another.

The earliest minute book of the Strabane Presbytery, covering the period 1717–40, reveals that it dealt with a variety of matters relating to the members of the congregations within its bounds (CR3/26/2/1). For instance, in December 1718 John Alison came before the

Presbytery desiring a certificate testifying to his credentials as a good Presbyterian as he was preparing to emigrate. Presbytery decided not to issue him with one until just before he was ready to leave, and then only if his behaviour was considered satisfactory. The following extracts are all from October 1730 and concern a range of issues associated with the marriages of Presbyterians:

> John Murdagh & Jane Sample appeared & said John insisted on his having married to Jane & produced as witnesses, Mrs Wilson of Strabane & his own sister Janet, who were present in Mrs Wilson's Stable when they were married by a Popish Priest & solemnly declared they heard the priest marry them & that when the priest asked Jane Sample if she was willing to take John Murdagh for her husband, she answered, she was willing. Jane Sample confesses she went away with an intention to marry said John Murdagh and that she bedded with him … the Presbytery … give it as their judgement that the marriage is valid in the sight of God & appoint Mr Homes to confer with Jane Sample and her father, and advise her to live with John Murdagh as her husband …

> John Patterson & Mary Atchinson appeared; it being alleged that they were married before John Hemphill her former husband (who went to America) was dead; they [stated] that they were informed John Hemphill was dead & they took it for granted that he was dead, else they would not have married … this Presbytery charitably believes they thought John Hemphill was dead, yet in the eyes of the world it appears too like adultery …

> John Caldwell and Grizzel Johnson appeared as appointed & both confess they were married by a Popish Priest but are not willing to live together. The Presbytery having heard them, exhorted them to be reconciled and live together in love and with the fear of God …

From the latter part of the seventeenth century through to 1840 the Synod of Ulster was the highest authority in the Presbyterian Church in Ulster. It met once a year, usually in June, and was composed of representatives from every congregation in each of the presbyteries. To a large extent the minutes deal with matters of procedure within the Church. Occasionally, however, information of real genealogical value will be recorded as the following example shows. Plans to form a new congregation at Coagh on the boundary between counties Londonderry and Tyrone were resisted strongly by two existing congregations in this area, but in 1709 the Synod of Ulster ruled in favour of the people of Coagh. The entry in the Synod minutes provides considerable detail on the bounds of this congregation and its founding members:

> That the new Erection at Coagh, made by the late Committee at Ballenderry, July 20th, 1708, for that People, stand & continue a distinct Congregation, bounded as follows, viz:—that Wm McMullen & Neighbours in Millinaho, Thos Bell and Neighbours in Tirkvillan, Rich: Rankin & Neigbours in Tirkvillan, John McCreigh in Drumady, Wm Vans & Hugh Fleck in Achavan, Richd McGau in Ballynargan, Jas Dun & his Neighbours in Inniskillin, Thos McCord & Moses Redman in Edruna, Alexr Mitchell in Liscasy, James McCord in the Moor, Claud Rolan in Ballynahone, James Johnston & Andw Ferguson in Drummullan, at the little Bridge, James McKee & Wm Hamilton in Ballydally, Jas Hogg and John McKee in Ballygurch, Wm Aikin & John Barnet in Ballycogly, & from that to the Logh by Ballyronan, and all these People, and all these within those Bounds, be the new Erection of Coagh, and apply to the Meeting of Tyrone to plant them.[4]

At different times, issues concerning Presbyterian marriages occupied the Synod's attention. For instance, at the meeting of Synod in 1716 the excommunication of Presbyterians by the Church of Ireland on account of their marriages was highlighted (see Chapter 4 for more on Presbyterians and marriage). Those named specifically were John Chamberlain, James Cresswell and John Warden of Fahan, County Donegal, James Ball of Ballymoney, County Antrim, and Nivin Twynan and William Curry of Donacloney and James Martin of Tullylish, all County Down.[5]

Disputes over the siting of meeting houses also came before the higher courts of Presbyterianism. At the meeting of the Burgher Secession Synod in August 1788 the matter of the location of a new meeting house for the congregation of Clonaneese was discussed. The issue had divided the congregation with a minority section, referred to as being from the 'Lower part', wanting to remain on the existing site as against the wishes of the majority from the 'Upper part'. The Synod heard from representatives of the two sections: Francis Wilson, John

Wilson and Samuel Dickson from the 'Lower part'; and William Bell, James McMullan, James Reid and James Farquer from the 'Upper part'. On a vote the members of Synod supported the majority section of the congregation.[6] The minority rejected the decision of Synod and withdrew from this body and formed a new congregation – Lower Clonaneese – which joined the Antiburgher Secession Synod.

6.3 Other Presbyterian bodies

Within the General Assembly and the highest courts of the other Presbyterian churches there were various boards and committees dealing with a range of areas of responsibility, such as missions, or which were charged with investigating specific issues or developing particular initiatives. Some of the records created by these bodies are in the public domain, but many are not. Found among the records of the Magee University College Presbyterian Trust in PRONI is the minute book of the General Assembly's Committee on Temperance, 1892–1932 (MPT/1/4/1). With regard to the Reformed Presbyterian Church, PRONI has some records of the Trustees of Synod, including a minute book for the years 1870–1930 and an accounts ledger, 1870–76 (CR5/5/A/4).

Presbyterian Orphan Society

Now called the Presbyterian Children's Society, the Presbyterian Orphan Society was founded in 1866. The two key figures in its formation were Rev. William Johnston, minister of the Townsend Street congregation in Belfast, and Wilberforce Arnold, a medical doctor. While focused primarily on orphans from Presbyterian families, support was provided to children from other denominational backgrounds. In order for a child to receive support from the Society he or she had to be 'elected'. Elections were held twice a year and applications for support had to be signed by 'the surviving parent, nearest relative or friend (when there is such), and by a minister of the Presbyterian congregation in which the deceased parents worshipped'.

PRONI has an extensive collection of records relating to the work of the Society (CR3/50/A). The items include minute books, 1865–1990; registers of orphans, 1866–1961; applications for election as orphans under the Society, 1901–36; roll of members, 1866–73; annual reports, 1866–2001; cash books, 1866–79, payment books, 1893–1971; and a damp press copy out-letter book, 1893–1900. The registers of orphans include: name of the child, date of birth, occupation of father, congregation with which associated, date of 'election' (when it was agreed to provide support), the amount provided and the date the child was removed from the register. Later volumes also include information on the Johnston Memorial Home/Training School (see below) and details of apprenticeships. The collection is closed to the public. All requests to access the collection should be directed to the Private Records section in PRONI.

Some other records relating to the Presbyterian Orphan Society in PRONI, mainly in connection with Greenwell Street Presbyterian Church in Newtownards, are listed under D1195. These include grants for orphans in connection with Greenwell Street, 1914–24. There is also an apprenticeship agreement between Samuel Shaw of Conlig and Henry Miskelly, tailor, Newtownards, and the Governors of the Presbyterian Orphan Society (D1195/4/10). Another document in PRONI is a 'Corrected List' of applicants for election, November 1891 (T2547/3). Rev. Prof. John M. Barkley authored a volume on the Society's centenary: *The Presbyterian Orphan Society, 1866–1966* (1966). A more recent history is Paul Gray, *Putting Children First – From Presbyterian Orphan Society to Presbyterian Children's Society* (2016). See also Paul Gray, 'In between the War and the Workhouse – Women assisted by the Presbyterian Orphan Society during the First World War', *BPHSI*, vol. 40 (2016).

PRONI also holds minute books, 1889–1985, and a cash book, 1887–92, of the Johnston Memorial Training Home (later known as the Johnston Memorial Training School), which was opened by the Presbyterian Orphan Society in 1888 in Hopefield Avenue, Belfast, to provide training in domestic service for girls supported by the Society (CR3/50/B). Its records are also closed and permission to access them should be made to the Private Records section in PRONI.

Other benevolent organisations

Several funds were established to assist retired ministers and their families. In the eighteenth century a fund was established by the Synod of Ulster to support ministers' widows and orphans and the names of beneficiaries are given in the printed minutes of Synod. In 1799 the Route Presbytery named those receiving assistance from this fund as:

Mrs Gasten, Mrs Smylie (they believe) as the last accounts they had of her she lived in the Isle of Man, Mrs Elder, Mrs Smyth, Mrs Hamilton, Mrs McMullan, Mrs Simson, family of Mr Douglas, & Mrs Davis, if alive, now residing in America.[7]

Minutes of the Aged and Infirm Ministers' Fund, 1890–1947, are in PHSI. PRONI has the minute books, 1873–1979, and cash books, 1872–1980, of the Society for Orphans of Ministers and Missionaries (CR3/50/C); these records are closed and permission to access them should be made to the Private Records section in PRONI. Other benevolent bodies of the Presbyterian Church include the Presbyterian Widows' Fund Association and the Secession Widows' Fund. PRONI holds annual reports of the former for 1934–47 and for the latter for 1935–48 (CR3/46/5/B).

Evangelical, educational and social organisations

Over the centuries Presbyterians have been involved in many different bodies. Some of these have been specifically Presbyterian in focus and officially under the auspices of the Presbyterian Church, though others have been non-denominational. It is not the purpose of this section to deal exhaustively with this subject, but to highlight a few examples of the Presbyterian involvement in such organisations. For example, Presbyterians played important or leading roles in several organisations with a focus on evangelism in working class areas of rapidly expanding towns and cities. A non-denominational Town Mission in Belfast was founded in 1827, which in 1843 was reorganised as a specifically Presbyterian body in connection with the General Assembly (after Belfast was given city status in 1888 the organisation was renamed the Belfast City Mission). Outreach work by Rev. Henry Montgomery on the Shankill Road in Belfast led to the founding of the Shankill Road Mission, which became a congregation in 1907.

The Londonderry City Mission was established in 1830 and though it too was a non-denominational body, Presbyterians played important roles in its work. The records of the Londonderry City Mission are in the Presbyterian Historical Society. The Bible and Colportage Society of Ireland was formed in the late 1850s with one of the co-founders being Rev. James McCosh, a Scotsman who at that time was a professor at Queen's College Belfast and was very active in various Presbyterian initiatives. The first annual meeting of the Society was held in May Street Presbyterian Church, Belfast, on 9 March 1859. PRONI holds a minute book of this Society for the years 1872–1909 (D2816/1). A transcription of the diary of Rev. Anthony McIntyre of the Domestic Mission to the Poor of Belfast, a Non-Subscribing Presbyterian organisation, 1853–6, is available in the PRONI eCatalogue (D1558/2/3).

The nineteenth century also witnessed the formation of a number of organisations aimed at providing social, educational and sporting activities for the young men and women of the Presbyterian Church. While some of these bodies were linked closely with a specific congregation, others brought together Presbyterians from a wider area. PRONI has records of several Presbyterian Young Men's Associations including: minute book of Ballymoney with an attendance record at the back of the volume, 1863–76 (D3350/1); minute books of Bessbrook, 1883–95 (D2826/66); and minute book of Loughbrickland, which includes a membership list and accounts, 1864–71 (T3628/1). The Central Presbyterian Association (CPA) was formed in Belfast in 1882 and the first half century of its history is told in Robert Johnston, *The Story of the Central Presbyterian Association, Belfast, 1882–1932* (1932). The CPA had its own Camera Club and minute books and other items relating to it for the years 1912–63 are in PRONI (D4005). Among other organisations, Presbyterians in Londonderry formed the City of Derry Presbyterian Working Men's Institute in 1883; for more on it, see *City of Derry Working Men's Institute. Jubilee Book 1883–1933* (1933).

Notes

[1] Both books were reprinted in 1978 as *Roots of Presbyterianism in Donegal.*

[2] For a more detailed look at the work of presbytery, see Barkley, *Short History of the Presbyterian Church,* chapter 4.

[3] McFarland, *Maghera,* p. 171.

[4] *RGSU,* vol. 1, p. 176.

[5] Ibid., p. 412.

[6] Fleck, *Clonaneese,* pp 42–3.

[7] *RGSU,* vol. 3, p. 219.

7

Presbyterian ministers

I was born at Brigh, near Stewartstown, in the county of Tyrone, A.D.
1802 ... By my father, the late Rev. Thomas M'Kay, I possess Celtic
origins; his grandfather, Alexander M'Kay, of Convoy ... was son to
Hugh M'Kay, of Rea, in the northern highlands of Scotland ...

Rev. William Kennedy McKay[1]

The minister (also known as the pastor or clergyman) was the key
figure in the congregation, the man – until the latter part of the
twentieth century Presbyterian ministers in Ireland were exclusively
male – with the responsibility for conducting public worship, chairing
meetings of the Session, visiting the sick, the aged and the infirm, and
much else besides. Beyond his own congregation, the minister was
required to attend the regular meetings of presbytery and the annual
meeting of Synod/General Assembly. He may also have been given the
care of a neighbouring congregation during a ministerial vacancy. As
leaders of their communities, ministers exercised a significant
influence in their respective localities, often providing a voice to local
grievances and campaigning for political reform, some even holding
elected office. A few led portions of their congregations to America.
Many people have an ancestor or at least someone in the family tree
who was a Presbyterian minister. This chapter looks at different
sources for studying ministers and highlights how the personal records
of clergymen can also be of assistance in researching not only their
own families, but also members of their congregations.

7.1 Presbyterian *Fasti*

Biographical information on Presbyterian ministers – mainly those who served in the Synod of Ulster – from the early seventeenth century through to 1840 can be found in *Fasti of the Irish Presbyterian Church, 1613–1840*. The collation of these details had been started by Rev. James McConnell who wished to produce something along the lines of the *Fasti Ecclesiae Scoticanae* originated by Rev. Hew Scott. McConnell died in 1922 and his work was continued by his son Rev. Samuel G. McConnell. Additional editorial work was carried out principally by Rev. David Stewart, who acknowledged that the work of the McConnells had been 'tedious and exacting'. The first three parts were published originally in the *Genealogists' Magazine*, before the entire work, divided into 12 parts in all, was issued by the Presbyterian Historical Society in 1951 (only 250 copies were printed). Part I of the *Fasti*, covering the years 1613–41, is available on the PHSI website (members only).

The typical data provided for each minister are: place of birth; family background, e.g. father's name and occupation; educational achievements; when and by which presbytery licensed; date and place of ordination; pastorates; date of death; and family, e.g. wife and children. Of course, gaps in the records mean not all of these details are known for every minister, such as the name of his father or information on his own family. Several paragraphs of biographical information are given for some seventeenth-century ministers, such as Robert Blair, James Hamilton and John Livingston. In most cases, however, the information provided is more limited. The following is a fairly typical entry for an eighteenth-century minister:

> BROWN, JOHN; 1st s. of James Brown, merchant, Coagh; bro. of Jas Brown, Connor; educ. Glas.; MA 1757; lic. Tyrone Pres.; ord. Waterford, cir., 1761; mar. dau. of Rev. John Mairs, Wood St, Dublin; d. 1775.

Other details that might appear include if a minister was suspended or deposed. If he emigrated to America or another part of the world the date of his departure might be given along with details of where he ministered. For those who emigrated, see Rev. David Stewart's *Fasti of the American Presbyterian Church: Treating of Ministers of Irish*

Origin who Laboured in America During the Eighteenth Century (1943), which is available on the PHSI website (members only). Further biographical information was published as *Fasti of the General Assembly of the Presbyterian Church in Ireland, 1840–1910*, compiled by John M. Barkley, and issued in three parts by the PHSI (1986–7). Biographical data on ministers since 1910 is held by the Presbyterian Historical Society.

Brief biographical sketches of Secession clergymen appear in *Fasti of Seceder Ministers Ordained or Installed in Ireland 1746–1948*, arranged and edited by W. D. Bailie and L. S. Kirkpatrick, published by the Presbyterian Historical Society in 2005. Largely the work of Rev. Prof. Adam Loughridge, brief biographical details of ministers of the Reformed Presbyterian Church are included in *The Covenanters in Ireland: A History of the Congregations* (2010). Also included are biographical details of Irish-born ministers in the Reformed Presbyterian Church of Scotland and the Reformed Presbyterian Church of North America, as well as the ministers of the short-lived Eastern Reformed Presbyterian Synod of Ireland. Brief details of ministers of the Church of Scotland who served in Ireland are included in *Fasti Ecclesiae Scoticanae*, vol. 7 (1928).

7.2 Family background

Some ministers were more conscious of their roots than others. Rev. William Kennedy McKay, who introduced this chapter and who was ordained minister of First Portglenone in 1826, was fascinated by his lineage. Rev. John Livingston, who became minister of Killinchy in 1630, was aware that his great-grandfather had been killed at the Battle of Pinkie, fought between the Scots and the English in 1547. On the other hand, Rev. James Morgan, who spent most of his ministry in Fisherwick Place, Belfast, confessed in his autobiography: 'I know little of [my family] history, and cannot trace it farther back than to my great-grandfather Morgan, on the one side, and my grandfather Collins, on the other.'[2] Some ministers were not even sure when they were born. Rev. Josias Wilson, who ministered in Donegore before emigrating to America, was unsure whether he was born in 1766 or 1769 (see below for more on him). Likewise Rev. John Wray of Convoy believed that he was 'supposed to be born the 27th of February, 1793 or 1795'.[3]

Various studies have analysed the background, education and careers of Presbyterian ministers in Ireland. Robert Whan devoted Chapter 1 of his book, *The Presbyterians of Ulster, 1680–1730* (2013) to the clergy. He notes that of the 303 ministers who were active in Ulster between 1680 and 1729 56% had been born in Ulster and 29% in Scotland (of the remainder, 1% were from England, 1% were from an unspecified location in Ireland, and the place of origin of the rest is not known). However, it was not until the final decade of the seventeenth century that the number of ministers known to have been born in Ireland outnumbered those born in Scotland. The social background is known for only around a quarter of the 303 ministers and of these the great majority were 'sons of the manse'. Whan also notes that nearly 60% of ministers ordained in the period 1640–1729 served as pastor of only one congregation, while another 23% ministered in two. For a look at the role of pastors in the 1700s, see J. M. Barkley, 'The Presbyterian minister in eighteenth-century Ireland', in J. L. M. Haire et al., *Challenge and Conflict: Essays in Irish Presbyterian History and Doctrine* (1981).

An analysis of ministers in the 1800s is provided by Kenneth D. Brown, 'Life after death: a preliminary survey of the Irish Presbyterian ministry in the nineteenth century', *Irish Economic and Social History*, vol. 22 (1995), pp 49–63. Brown's study draws primarily on the data contained in the *Fasti of the General Assembly of the Presbyterian Church in Ireland, 1840–1910*. In comparing the place of birth of ministers in the 1840s with the 1890s, he finds that the number of ministers born in Ireland exclusive of Ulster rose from 1% to 9%. Of those whose careers began in the 1840s 74% had only one pastorate, while this figure had dropped to 41.3% for those beginning their ministries in the 1890s. In his book, *The Presbyterian College, 1853–1953* (1953), Robert Allen noted that 76 of the first hundred students 'came from the land' (p. 332). However, in the latter 1800s this proportion had dropped to 52%. He also found that just over 12% of students were the sons of ministers.

7.3 Ministerial income

The minister's stipend (or salary) was paid by members of the congregation chiefly in the form of pew rents, a subject looked at in more detail in the next chapter. In some congregations the minister was expected to collect his own stipend, though in most congregations this task was given eventually to one or more 'collectors'. For example, until 1818 – nearly 30 years into his ministry – the minister of Kilraughts, Rev. Matthew Elder, had to collect his own stipend. In the spring of 1818 Alexander McIlhatton was appointed the collector of the stipend in Kilraughts and it was agreed that he would receive £3 for every £50 collected.[4] The way in which a congregation supported a minister was not limited to monetary payments. Many rural ministers were provided with a farm and so many days of labour by the members of his congregation. In 1700 the members of the congregation of Larne and Kilwaughter offered to purchase a horse to encourage a minister to settle with them.[5] Looking at the records of the Laggan Presbytery in the late seventeenth century, we find that in 1673 the members of the congregation of Donagheady offered to build a house for their pastor, Rev. John Hamilton, on a site of his choosing. By the following year a house had been provided and the congregation promised:

> To keep him free in that house, and to give him beside the house & garden an acre of meadow & two acres of corn & grass for a horse & two or three cows free & as much more of the land for payment for his use as he pleases (MIC637/6).

It was only in the Victorian era that the practice of a congregation building a manse for the use of the minister and his successors became widespread. PRONI holds a deed of 1852 concerning the leasing of 1 acre in the townland of Ballygallagh for 999 years at an annual rent of £4 for a manse for the congregation of First Ballyclare (D300/2/1/12/18). The following individuals were named as the trustees acting on behalf of the Ballyclare congregation: Alex. Woodside, Skilganaban; John Dundee, Bruslee; Alex. Galt, Doagh; Geo. Ledlie, Cogry; and Walter Simms, Ballywalter. The Young & Mackenzie archive in PRONI includes plans and papers for building Drumlough manse for Rev. John McClelland, c. 1880 (D2194/45/8).

Prior to 1871, a Presbyterian minister received a share of the *Regium Donum*. This was a government grant that had first been paid to Presbyterian ministers in 1672. In 1690 William III increased the amount on offer to £1,200 and it was raised to £1,600 in 1718 with an additional £400 for 'Protestant dissenters' in the south of Ireland.[6] There were further increases in the course of the eighteenth century and in 1784 it was extended to Secession ministers. (Covenanter ministers refused to have anything to do with the scheme.) In 1803, for the purpose of distributing the *Regium Donum*, Presbyterian congregations were divided into three classes according to the stipend that each paid. The *Regium Donum* for each of the classes was, in Irish currency, £100 (1st), £75 (2nd) and £50 (3rd). In 1809 the Seceders agreed to a similar arrangement with the classes set at £70, £50 and £40. In 1838 the grading system was ended and all ministers became entitled to £75 (with the rights of those in receipt of £100 preserved).[7]

Though much better known for disestablishing the Church of Ireland, the Irish Church Act of 1869 also had ramifications for Presbyterian ministers for it resulted in the withdrawal of the *Regium Donum*. Ministers were given the option of receiving an annuity for life (the value of which depended on their years of service), or commuting this to the benefit of the Presbyterian Church. If they chose the latter, as nearly all did, the Church received a bonus of 12 per cent. The income from the Commutation Fund was transferred to a newly created fund, the Sustentation Fund, which was bolstered by contributions from congregations.

Many clergymen were able to supplement their income through teaching (see Chapter 10). Few were as well off as Rev. Dr Henry Montgomery. In 1854 he provided the following information on his annual income in a parliamentary return: for teaching in Royal Belfast Academical Institution – £150; in 'pew rents, or money stipend' from his congregation of Dunmurry (in the Remonstrant Synod) – £69 9s. 1d.; from the *Regium Donum* – £92 6s. 2d.; as the distributor of *Regium Donum* to the ministers of the Remonstrant Synod and Presbytery of Antrim – £230 (including an allowance for stamps, postages, stationery etc). In addition, his congregation provided him with a 'pleasant manse and farm' worth *c.* £60 per annum.[8] The overwhelmingly majority of ministers subsisted on considerably less than this and many felt that they lived quite impoverished lives. Financial difficulties were major reasons for the departure of ministers to America and elsewhere.

7.4 Ministers' personal papers, diaries, sermons, etc

The personal papers of ministers can be extremely illuminating, not only on themselves and their families, but also on their congregations. At times it is hard to draw a clear dividing line between personal and congregational records since the minister himself generated many of the latter. However, such items as diaries, memorandum books and sermon notes can certainly be considered among the minister's personal papers. A number of diaries kept by ministers survive and are in the public domain. One of the earliest is the diary of William Holmes (or Homes), who was born in Donaghmore parish, County Donegal. As a young man he travelled to New England, but returned to Ireland and was ordained minister of Strabane in 1692. In 1714 Holmes resigned as minister of Strabane and again emigrated to New England where he became pastor of a congregation in Chilmark, Martha's Vineyard. His diary is in the Maine Historical Society; the Congregational Library & Archives in Boston provides online access to a digital copy of it.[9] While the covering dates of the diary are given as 1715–47, there is some valuable material from his time in Strabane, including details of his own family, unusual occurrences, and descriptions of the deaths of some people in the locality.

Another volume belonging to a Presbyterian minister of this era to travel across the Atlantic is the memorandum book, c. 1728–40, of Rev. Archibald Maclaine, minister of Banbridge from 1720 to his death in 1740. The volume includes some personal family records and commentary on contemporary events, including emigration and theological discussions. There are some additional entries by his son Archibald who emigrated to America in 1750. The memorandum book is in the Wilson Library, University of North Carolina at Chapel Hill (MS 2313), and there is a digitised copy on university's website.[10]

The Presbyterian Historical Society of Ireland holds the personal papers of many ministers including the diary of Rev. John Kennedy of Benburb, which provides immense detail on the life of this minister and his congregation between 1723 and 1737. Kennedy noted, for example, pastoral visits to members of his congregation and recorded details of baptisms, marriages and funerals that he had conducted. For instance, on 20 January 1726 Kennedy visited Andrew and Widow Trimble, married Dick Tinsly and Agnes Paton, called with Jo. McGee, and finally that day baptised William Campbell's child. The value of this diary for anyone researching an ancestor who belonged to Benburb Presbyterian Church cannot be overstated for registers of baptisms and marriages of the congregation do not begin until the nineteenth century (in fact, there are no baptism registers until the 1870s). An edition of this diary is in preparation by the Presbyterian Historical Society. The PHSI also holds the common-place book of Rev. Samuel Barber of Rathfriland, which includes records of the marriages in his congregation from 1782 to 1811 and a list of the Rathfriland Volunteers in 1781, as well as various other jottings.

There have been few more assiduous record-keepers among the Presbyterian ministry than Rev. Robert Magill of Antrim. Born in Broughshane in 1788, and a witness to the local events of the 1798 Rebellion, Robert Magill was ordained minister of Antrim Presbyterian Church (known as Millrow) in 1820. He remained minister of this congregation until his death in 1839. Magill was an incredible record-keeper. Extraordinarily detailed registers of the congregation were maintained during his ministry and his fabulous family record book is noted in Chapter 5. Magill also kept a diary or daily journal from 1821 until just before he died. Most of these diaries (1821–4 and 1831–7), along with other documents, including an autobiography of the minister, are found within the papers of the Young family of Belfast in PRONI (D2930/9); Magill's only surviving child Sarah married the architect Robert Young. The diary of 1838–9 is also in PRONI (CR3/2/C/1). The entries in the diary of 1827 and 1828 were reproduced in James G. Kenny, *As the Crow Flies over Rough Terrain: Incorporating the Diary 1827/1828 and More of a Divine* (1988); this diary had been in private possession, but is now in the Presbyterian Historical Society.

The diary provides a phenomenal amount of information on Magill's congregation and the locality as well as a real insight into the day to day activities of an early nineteenth-century Presbyterian minister. The following observations on it are from Magill's entry in the *Dictionary of Irish Biography*:

> Its attention to detail is extraordinary: he notes the jobs of his parishioners, their time of death to the very minute, the names of his correspondents and visitors, the genealogy of everyone, and the price of everything. It attests to his constant, dutiful parish work and to a methodical, even obsessive, cataloguing mind and is of considerable historical interest.[11]

To take one date, 31 July 1827, as an example, Magill visited the families of Widow Moore, Mary Johnson, Mrs James Finlay, Thomas Anderson, John Orr, Widow John Orr, Anthony Roy, Adam Linn, Samuel Steel, David McQuillan, Widow Samuel Orr, Widow William Orr, William Kirkpatrick, Widow Kearney, Robert French, James Campbell, John Kirkpatrick, Robert Carson (and baptised Robert's son John, who had been born the day before), William Groves, Widow Greenlees, John Crawford and Alexander Black. He was provided with refreshments at the home of John Campbell, where he dined and drank tea; there was further tea-drinking with Widow William Orr. Finally that day he visited 'old Mr Reford'.

PRONI has a number of other collections of personal papers of Presbyterian ministers. For example, correspondence and papers of Rev. John Tennent and his family is listed under reference D1748. Tennent, a native of Scotland, was the minister of the Secession congregation of Roseyards in north County Antrim from 1751 to his death in 1808. His sons William, Robert and John became prominent figures in business and politics in Belfast. There is a significant collection of records relating to Rev. J. B. Armour (1841–1928), minister of Trinity Ballymoney from 1869 until his retirement in 1925. Catalogued under reference D1792, the documentation includes letters to and from Armour on a range of issues, as well as other material relating to his life and career. For more on Armour and this collection, including transcriptions of many of the letters, see the PRONI publication by J. R. B. McMinn: *Against the Tide: Rev. J. B. Armour, Irish Presbyterian Minister and Home Ruler 1869–1914* (1985). Some additional papers relating to Armour, including a family history written by his grandson, J. S. S. Armour, and a collection of photographs are catalogued under D4515.

PRONI also has the papers of W. R. Rodgers, who served as minister of Loughgall (also known as Cloveneden), from 1935 to 1946, before going on to become a major literary figure (D2833). Among the items concerning his ministry are the 'call' he received from the congregation of Loughgall, 1934; the minute book of the Cloveneden and District Victory Gift Fund of which Rodgers was chairman, 1944–5; and a printed inventory of the contents of Cloveneden manse, 1946. The papers of Rev. A. H. McElroy (1915–75) held by PRONI concern his career in the Non-Subscribing

Presbyterian Church and his involvement in Liberal politics in Northern Ireland (D3342). He served as minister of the Non-Subscribing Presbyterian Church in Newtownards from 1954 until his death.[12] The small collection of papers relating to his ministerial career includes articles, correspondence, and notes on and copies of sermons.

Ministerial diaries and personal papers are on deposit in other archives. It has been noted in Chapter 3 that papers of the clerical Bruce family are in the National Library of Ireland in Dublin (MSS 20,867–21,961), while the Manuscripts & Archives Research Library in Trinity College Dublin holds diaries covering the period 1792–95 that have been attributed to Rev. William Bruce (MSS 10,083–10,084).[13] The Cork City and County Archives has eight volumes of diaries of Rev. Dr Thomas Blakely (PR41), though these are mainly from before he became a minister in Cork. The Special Collections at Queen's University Belfast include the Allen Collection (MS 23), comprising the working papers of Rev. Robert Allen (1904–68), a Presbyterian minister and respected historian; the papers also contain material generated by another minister and historian, Rev. William Thomas Latimer (1842–1919), including extracts from original church records. The diary, 1861–71, of Rev. Randal McCollum of Glasleck is in Johnston Central Library, Cavan.

Sermons and sermon notes are available for a significant number of ministers. Among the earliest is the sermon notebook of Rev. Seth Drummond of Ramelton, 1705–07 (MIC1P/455). Other collections of sermons in PRONI include: four bundles of sermons of Rev. William Fletcher and Rev. Alexander Heron, successively ministers of Ballyroney Presbyterian Church, c. 1813–c. 1860 (CR3/30/1); and c. 100 sermons of the Rev. William Kennedy McKay, minister of First Portglenone, c. 1824–c. 1870 (D2594/3). PRONI also has a record book of sermons heard by Samuel A. Russell at First Antrim and elsewhere, 1885–1915 (CR3/2/C/3). Collections of sermons are also available in the Presbyterian Historical Society. It was often the case that sermons delivered on important occasions, such as at the meetings of the Synod of Ulster and at funerals of prominent individuals, were published.

7.5 Autobiographies and biographies

There is a long history of Presbyterian ministers in Ireland writing an autobiography. These were not necessarily intended to be distributed widely or even published. Robert Blair (1593–1666), who became minister of Bangor in 1623, opened his autobiography with these words:

> Having met with great variety and vicissitudes of conditions in my lifetime, and drawing now near to the close of it (my seventieth year being almost expired), and having had experience of the constant care and kindness of my unchangeable Lord, I think myself obliged to leave some notes concerning the chief passages that have occurred to me in my pilgrimage, that my wife and children, at least, might have these to be a memorial of the way that I kept in the world, and that they may be the better furnished to answer the calumnies and reproaches that have been, and possibly may be cast upon me; and that so much the more because this hath been often required from me by my near relations, and some others also.[14]

Another seventeenth-century autobiography of a minister who spent some time in Ireland is that of John Livingston (1603–72), who served in Killinchy in the 1630s. This was written while Livingston was in exile in Rotterdam 'for the use of my children'.[15] The writings of both Blair and Livingston are crucially important works for understanding the early development of Presbyterianism on this island. The National Library of Ireland has a manuscript copy of 'A true narrative of the most material passages of the life of the late Revd. Mr William Jacque, some time minister of the gospel in Dublin in Ireland, likewise at Clapham near London in England, and last at Kelso in Scotland, where he died … 1699' (MS 34,946). This had been 'Written by his own hand some time before his death, and transcribed at the request of … the Earle of Marchmount, Lord High Chancellour'.

In the eighteenth century Adam Blair (1718–90) wrote an autobiography, copies of which are in the Genealogical Office, a department of the National Library of Ireland (GO, MS 544), and in the Manuscripts & Archives Research Library of Trinity College Dublin (MS 6447a). The copy in TCD was transcribed from the original by Blair's great-great-grandson, the famous genealogist

Tenison Groves. Blair was born in Ballymoney and educated at Glasgow University. Because of his views on the issue of subscription to the Westminster Confession of Faith he was licensed by the non-subscribing Presbytery of Antrim. In 1748 he accepted a call to become minister of the congregation at Horse Leap, near Birr, Country Offaly (then King's County). His retirement was spent in Lisburn. TCD also holds a typed transcript of Blair's diary, 1752–90 (MS 6447).

Andrew Craig's autobiography, reproduced in the *Ulster Journal of Archaeology*, provides interesting information on his early life in Dehomed in the parish of Drumgooland, County Down, where he was born in 1754, his education both in Ireland and at Glasgow University and his early ministry, initially in Moira and then in Lisburn. The surviving manuscript breaks off suddenly in 1787.[16] The following extract concerns Craig's family background:

My father, Andrew Craig (born April, 1700), held a farm under Sir Arthur Hill ... This farm is now the property of my nephew, Andrew Craig. ... This farm was part of a much larger one possessed by my grandfather ... The family came, as I have heard, from the south of Scotland, from Kilmarnock, at what period I know not. ... My father was of an industrious, sober, and religious character, a Presbyterian, and a regular member of the congregation of Ballyroney. By his first wife he had two children, Elizabeth, who was married to Wm. Martin in the neighbourhood of Dromore, and James, who is now in America, in Ohio County, the father of a numerous family, and possessed of one thousand acres of land. They were both married before I was born. The family of my mother, whose maiden name was Rachel Martin, occupied a valuable farm in Cloughskelt, the adjoining townland. ... The family, I believe, was also from Scotland. My father was years older than my mother. She was but sixteen when she was married. They had ten children. Samuel, the eldest, married Margaret Irwin; Jane, Hans Hamilton; Mary, Alexander Porter; Joseph was a soldier in Strood's regiment, and was killed at Carrickfergus by the French who landed with Thurot [in 1760]. Rachel was married to Hugh Morrison, of Tanderagee; Sarah and Andrew died young; and Rose, now a widow, was married to Francis Steel, of Rathconnell, Co. Armagh. I was their ninth child and fourth son.

In addition to providing details about his own family background, a minister's autobiography can also furnish information about members of his congregation.[17] In 1828 Rev. James Morgan became the first pastor of Fisherwick Place, Belfast, where he remained until his death in 1873. His autobiography, *Recollections of My Life and Times* (1874), was published posthumously. In this extract Morgan writes about some of the members of Session in his congregation:

> Mr. Taylor is a most amiable and generous man, ready to every good work; Mr. M'Neill is a thoughtful, devout, constant, and conscientious member of Session, taking his part always in the best spirit. Mr. Workman, who died greatly lamented a short time ago, was like him. They were most intimate friends. Mr. Lytle is a most energetic, able, thoughtful, and helpful brother. He was Mayor of Belfast three successive years. Mr. Charles Finlay is my son-in-law – the most trusted friend I have ever had beyond my own house, and the most perfect man of whom I have ever had any knowledge. Mr. William Laird Finlay is his brother, and like him in all respects. His services to us are beyond all our commendation. These brothers are the nephews of Mr. Charles Thomson, and grandsons of one of the most venerable and admirable ministers that ever belonged to the Presbyterian Church – the late Rev. John Thomson, of Carnmoney. Mr. Lyle was one of the humblest, best, and most useful of men. He died some years ago. Mr. Guthrie is a wise, good, steadfast brother, always to be reckoned on and found in his place. John Murray was godly from his youth, and died at an early age at Rostrevor, where he was the principal founder of the congregation presided over by my son, the Rev. Thomas Morgan. Thomas M'Clure was a most consistent office-bearer while he remained with us, but he got a church built at Belmont, and went there (p. 76).

Congregational histories usually give considerable attention to the lives and careers of pastors. Of other works, two early volumes are Alexander McCreery, *The Presbyterian Ministers of Killileagh* (1875) and Thomas Hamilton (ed.), *Irish Worthies: A Series of Original Biographical Sketches of Eminent Ministers and Members of the Presbyterian Church in Ireland* (1875). The Presbyterian Historical Society has published numerous short biographies of prominent ministers either as standalone booklets or as articles in its *Bulletin*. For biographies of prominent Reformed Presbyterian ministers, see Rev.

Samuel Ferguson's *Brief Biographical Sketches of Some Covenanting Ministers Who Laboured During the Latter Half of the Eighteenth Century* (1898) and *Preachers of the Covenants*, edited by Trevor McCavery (2016). A number of Irish Presbyterian ministers have been of sufficient importance to merit a full length academic biography. For example, Rev. Isaac Nelson, minister of Donegall Road Presbyterian Church in Belfast, is the subject of a 2018 study by Daniel Ritchie, *Isaac Nelson: Radical Abolitionist, Evangelical Presbyterian, and Irish Nationalist*, published by Oxford University Press. The *Dictionary of Irish Biography* (9 vols, Cambridge, 2009) includes entries for more than 150 Presbyterian ministers – testimony to the impact these men had on their communities and further afield.

7.6 Presentations to ministers

On his retirement, move to another sphere of labour, or on reaching a milestone in his ministry, a minister was often presented with a special gift by the congregation and his friends. The National Library of Ireland has a manuscript entitled, 'Stanzas composed for the jubilee anniversary of the Rev. Robert Campbell's ministry, to be celebrated in Templepatrick, on Friday, July 23, 1847, by Rev. Hugh Hutton' (MS 35,141/9). An illuminated address was presented to Rev. William Bruce on the completion of his fiftieth year as minister of the First Presbyterian Church, Belfast, in 1862. This with the reply and signatures of members of the congregation is in the Ulster Museum (Acc. 475–1930, 398–1933).

Presentations to ministers were often reported in the press and a newspaper report might include the names of subscribers to the gift. For example, the *Strabane Morning Post* of 9 October 1832 published the address by the 'Members of the Presbyterian Congregation and other Inhabitants of Strabane' to Rev. William Mulligan, who was leaving the town to take up a professorship at Royal Belfast Academical Institution, and the minister's response to it. The address to Mulligan contained over 100 signatures. In some instances a memorial tablet was erected within the meeting house to a former minister. The records of First Ballymoney include an account book containing details of subscriptions for a memorial to Rev. Robert Park who died in 1876.

7.7 Ministers and emigration

Since the seventeenth century Presbyterian ministers from Ireland have been emigrating to all corners of the globe. The subject is a major one in itself and only a few comments can be made here. This discussion does not include those sent out as missionaries by the Presbyterian churches (see below for more on that) or those who emigrated as children or young men, but who went on to train as ministers in their new home. As already highlighted, the various *Fasti* of the Presbyterian churches provide details on the emigration of ministers. Much of the focus of Rankin Sherling's *The Invisible Irish: Finding Protestants in the Nineteenth-Century Migrations to America* (2016) is on the migration of Presbyterian ministers from Ulster to America from the late seventeenth century onwards and a consideration of what that can tell us about the broader story of the transatlantic movement of Presbyterians.

The first attempt to establish a colony of Presbyterians from Ireland in North America was in 1636 when the *Eagle Wing* set sail from Belfast Lough with 140 men, women and children on board. The ship had been built for a group of Presbyterian ministers who wanted to emigrate to New England where they hoped to enjoy religious freedom. Disappointingly for those on board, severe storms forced the vessel to return to Ireland. However, by the latter part of the 1600s Presbyterians, including ministers, were regularly sailing across the Atlantic. Reference has been made above to Rev. William Holmes and attention can also be drawn to Francis Makemie, the 'Father of American Presbyterianism', who left Donegal for Maryland in 1683. Very possibly in Makemie's company, William Trail, the minister of Lifford (Ballindrait) Presbyterian Church, also emigrated to Maryland in 1683. Surviving from 1706 is an address by a group of Presbyterians resident at New Castle, Delaware, but formerly members of Trail's congregation in County Donegal, appealing for a minister to be sent out by their mother church, lest 'we and our posterity [be] left as a prey to superstition and heresies' (T3762/1).

Presbyterian ministers were considered to be important drivers of emigration in the eighteenth century. A remarkable document created by Ulster Presbyterians is the petition bearing the date 26 March 1718, which was addressed to Samuel Shute, the Governor of Massachusetts and New Hampshire. This was signed by over 300

'Inhabitants of the North of Ireland' who expressed 'our sincere and hearty inclination to transport ourselves to that very excellent and renowned plantation' on being given 'suitable encouragement'. The petition, which is now in the custody of the New Hampshire Historical Society, was carried to Boston by Rev. William Boyd of Macosquin. How many of the signatories actually emigrated is not clear – of the nine Presbyterian ministers to sign it, not one left Ireland. The names of the signatories have been printed in C. K. Bolton, *Scotch-Irish Pioneers* (1910) (pp 324–30).

Two ministers who did lead sections of their congregation to New England in 1718 were Rev. James McGregor of Aghadowey and Rev. James Woodside of Dunboe. Other ministers involved in leading substantial numbers of people to America include Rev. Thomas Clark, minister of the Secession congregation of Cahans, County Monaghan, who, in 1764, led 300 people to New York. In 1772, the Reformed Presbyterian minister Rev. William Martin, whose meeting house was at Kellswater, near Ballymena led a major exodus of families, mainly from County Antrim, to South Carolina at a time when agrarian unrest was threatening the stability of the north of Ireland. A detailed study of this episode is Jean Stephenson, *Scotch-Irish Migration to South Carolina, 1772 (Rev. William Martin and His Five Shiploads of Settlers)* (1971). The transatlantic movement of Presbyterian ministers and licentiates around the time of the 1798 Rebellion is a major part of the study by Peter Gilmore, Trevor Parkhill and William Roulston, *Exiles of '98: Ulster Presbyterians and the United States* (2018).

The emigration of ministers continued in the nineteenth century and their destinations now included Australia, Canada and New Zealand. In 1807 Rev. Josias Wilson, formerly minister of the Secession congregation of Donegore, emigrated to America and became a pastor in Pennsylvania. He died in 1812. On New Year's Day 1806, when he was living in Ballymena, Wilson began to write his autobiography in which, among other things, he revealed his sympathy for the United Irishmen. Though he never joined the organisation, he took an oath not to inform on its members. Unfortunately, Wilson terminated his autobiography before the start of the rebellion in 1798. Wilson carried his autobiography to the New World and, having been passed down through his family, it is now in the Library & Archives of York County History Center, Pennsylvania.[18] A work penned in 1809, likewise for the benefit of his children, was published in Belfast in 1825: *Advice Written by the Late Rev. Josias Wilson, For the Use of His Children, York County, Pennsylvania, 1809* (copy in the Linen Hall Library).

Of individuals who emigrated in the 1900s the example may be given of Rev. Dr Robert Magill (1871–1930), a native of Drumlee, County Down, who was ordained pastor of Maghera Presbyterian Church in 1900. In 1903 he resigned Maghera to move to Canada to take up a position as Professor of Systematic Theology and Apologetics at the Presbyterian College in Halifax, Nova Scotia, becoming principal of the college in 1907. In 1909 he moved to Dalhousie University, also in Nova Scotia, to become Professor of Philosophy. Having held a number of other public appointments, in 1912 he became the first Chief Commissioner of the Board of Grain Commissioners for Canada. Further positions followed and he came to be considered the greatest authority on the grain trade in the dominion. Some of Magill's papers are in Library & Archives Canada, including a photograph of the church and manse at Maghera (R2507-0-7-E).

7.8 Ministers as overseas missionaries

Many Presbyterian ministers, as well as numerous other Presbyterians, have served in the mission field, both at home and abroad. A native of County Monaghan, Rev. Hope Masterton Waddell (1804–95) has been called the first Presbyterian from Ireland to serve as an overseas missionary. He worked under the auspices of the Scottish Missionary Society, initially in Jamaica and later in Calabar, Nigeria. He recounted his endeavours in *Twenty-nine Years in the West Indies and Central Africa: a Review of Missionary Work and Adventure, 1829–1858* (1863). One of the first resolutions of the new General Assembly of the Presbyterian Church in Ireland in 1840 was to send two recently ordained ministers, James Glasgow and Alexander Kerr, to India. This was the beginning of the denomination's formal engagement with overseas mission work. Subsequently, the Presbyterian Church sent missionaries to China and other parts of the world. Lists of PCI missionaries to India, China and other countries can be found on the PHSI website (members only).

The Presbyterian Historical Society has documents and artefacts relating to a number of Presbyterian missionaries. For example, there is a copy of the diary of Rev. Robert Montgomery, who was sent as a missionary to India in 1842 and spent a short time in Porbandar. There are also diaries and correspondence of Rev. Andrew Weir who worked in Manchuria, China, from 1899 to 1933. The Presbyterian Mission Archive in the Gamble Library of Union Theological College contains a broad range of items relating to the work of missionaries at home and abroad. PRONI holds a number of collections concerning missionary work. These include papers of Rev. Alexander Crawford, a Scotsman who served as a missionary in India before becoming minister of First Randalstown in 1836. There is also correspondence relating to Dr James Campbell, Presbyterian missionary in the New Hebrides, 1902–12 (D1864). PRONI also has a collection of papers of Amy Carmichael, who was baptised in Ballycopeland Presbyterian Church in 1868, and went on to establish the Dohnavur Fellowship in India (D4061).

With regard to publications on missionaries, the PCI Board of Mission Overseas has produced a book entitled, *Into All the World – A History of the Overseas Work of the Presbyterian Church in Ireland 1840–1990*, edited by Jack Thompson. Bill Addley has written biographies of Dr James Glasgow and Dr Jack Weir for the Presbyterian Historical Society. Another PHSI publication is Salters Sterling's biography of Dr Thomas McCurdy Barker. Mark O'Neill is the author of *Frederick – The Life of My Missionary Grandfather in Manchuria* (2012). For the mission work of Covenanters, see Samuel R. Archer, *A Brief History of the Irish Mission of the Reformed Presbyterian Church* (1970). Isobel Lytle's book, *James Martin: Pioneer Medical Missionary in Antioch* (2003), looks at the life of a Reformed Presbyterian missionary in Syria, 1871–1924.

Notes

[1] *Belfast Newsletter*, 17 June 1836; in this article McKay goes into great detail on his family history.

[2] James Morgan, *Recollections of My Life and Times: An Autobiography* (1874), p. 1.

3 Mullin, *Convoy*, p. 141.

4 Blair, *Kilraughts*, pp 54–5.

5 Porter, *Larne and Kilwaughter*, p. 24.

6 Holmes, *Our Irish Presbyterian Heritage*, pp 58–9.

7 Barkley, *Short History of the Presbyterian Church*, p. 27.

8 *Accounts and Papers ... Ireland*, vol. 58 (1858), pp 406–07.

9 http://www.congregationallibrary.org/nehh/series2/HomesWilliam. See also 'Diary of Rev. William Homes of Chilmark, Martha's Vineyard, 1689–1746', *New England Historical and Genealogical Register*, 48 (1894), pp 446–53; 49 (1895), pp 413–16; 50 (1896), pp 155–66.

10 https://finding-aids.lib.unc.edu/02313.

11 *Dictionary of Irish Biography*, vol. 6, p. 254. See also John Erskine, 'The Reverend Robert Magill: a bibliographical view, 1827–1828', in John Gray and Wesley McCann (ed.), *An Uncommon Bookman: Essays in Honour of J. R. R. Adams* (1996) and W. D. Bailie, 'The Rev. Robert Magill and his journals', *BPHSI*, vol. 23 (1994).

12 Gordon Gillespie, *Albert H. McElroy: The Radical Minister, 1915–1975* (1985).

13 Material relating to the Bruce ministers is also available in PRONI (T3041), including letters from Rev. Michael Bruce of Holywood to his cousin James Traill in Killyleagh, 1717–35.

14 T. McCrie (ed.), *The Life of Mr Robert Blair, Containing his Autobiography from 1593 to 1636* (1848), p. [3].

15 *A Brief Historical Relation, of the Life of Mr John Livingston* (1727).

16 [A. A. Campbell] 'An autobiographical sketch of Andrew Craig, 1754–1833. Presbyterian minister of Lisburn', *UJA*, 2nd series, vol. 14 (1908), pp 10–15, 51–5.

17 For a discussion of how little a minister's biography or autobiography might reveal about his family, see Janice Holmes, 'The "absence" of family in 19th-century Irish Presbyterian clerical biographies', in Anders Jarlert (ed.), *Spiritual and Ecclesiastical Biographies. Research, Results, and Reading* (2017), pp 105–20.

18 Unpublished paper by Richard K. MacMaster titled, 'Josias Wilson and the uses of autobiography'.

8

Presbyterian places of worship and burial

But now the old meeting house shows itself through the trees. ... Here it is! The same long, low stone building in the shape of a 'T,' and roofed with straw thatch, just as I remember to have seen it sixty-four years ago.

Thomas Mellon on visiting the old Mountjoy meeting house in County Tyrone in 1882[1]

8.1 Places of worship

Historically, the term 'meeting house' has been applied to Presbyterian places of worship, though in more recent times the word 'church' has been used. The earliest Presbyterians in Ireland met for worship in parish churches, i.e. churches which were officially under the control of the Church of Ireland. Thus, Robert Blair conducted services in Bangor Abbey, while Robert Cunningham preached in the parish church in Holywood. During the Cromwellian period of the 1650s many Presbyterians served as parish ministers and preached in parish churches. This ended with the Restoration and the expulsion of Presbyterian ministers in 1661. For the next few years larger gatherings of Presbyterians tended to take place in the open air. Specifically Presbyterian places of worship began to be erected from the late 1660s onwards. The first meeting houses were simple halls. Possibly the earliest surviving example, though it has not been used as such for over a century, is in Ramelton, County Donegal. The Old Meeting House, as it is known, comprises two adjoining halls, one shorter than the other; the longer hall seems to be the older and may date from *c.* 1700.[2]

The Old Meeting House in Ramelton stands in Back Lane, an appropriate illustration of the fact that for a long time to come Presbyterian places of worship tended to be located in less conspicuous rural areas or on the edge of towns. Occasionally there was hostility to the construction of these buildings from the Anglican establishment. In 1669, for example, the recently erected meeting house in Bangor was demolished on the orders of the Countess of Clanbrassil. A number of landlords used their powers to thwart the construction of meeting houses. For instance, in a lease issued by Ralph Gore for land in County Fermanagh there was a clause forbidding the tenant from allowing the construction of a place of worship or dwelling of any 'Popish Priest or any Preacher or Teacher dissenting from the Church of Ireland' (D580/34). Nonetheless, a considerable number of Presbyterian meeting houses were built with the approbation of local landowners.

Lacking wealthy patrons, most eighteenth-century Presbyterian congregations did not build architecturally distinguished places of worship and in general their meeting houses were plain structures, both internally and externally. What came to be regarded as the characteristic form of a Presbyterian meeting house was the T-plan with the pulpit positioned midway along the long wall. This arrangement reflected the Presbyterian emphasis on the preaching of the Word and provided a practical solution to the accommodation needs of sizeable congregations. Frequently galleries were added in each of the arms to give even more seating space and these were usually accessed via external staircases. Dating from 1787, the meeting house at Rademon, County Down, is a good example of a substantial two-storey, rubble-built, T-plan building; it is impressive for its scale and features a Classical surround to the door, but it is essentially a vernacular structure.

The involvement of professional architects in designing Presbyterian meeting houses began in the second half of the eighteenth century though tended to be restricted to the wealthier congregations.[3] The most distinguished eighteenth-century Presbyterian meeting house in Ireland is the First Presbyterian Church in Belfast. Designed by Roger Mulholland and opened in 1783, this handsome meeting house is elliptical in plan with a gallery supported on Corinthian columns.[4] No less a figure than John Wesley described it as 'the completest place of worship I have ever seen.' Fine early nineteenth-century examples of Classical churches are those at Ballykelly and Banagher in County Londonderry, both of which were built with support from the local landlord, the Fishmongers' Company of London. Opened in 1835, Castlereagh Presbyterian Church is believed to be the first Presbyterian meeting house with a belfry. It was one of a number of high quality Presbyterian places of worship designed by John Millar. Another was Portaferry Presbyterian Church, regarded as one of the finest Neoclassical buildings in Ireland.

Even with this very obvious preference for Classicism, which continued well into the nineteenth century, by the mid 1820s the influence of the Gothic Revival was leaving its mark on Presbyterian architecture in Ireland. A new meeting house in Drogheda of 1826–8 resembled a miniature version of King's College Chapel, Cambridge. Gothic architecture became increasingly popular during the Victorian period and was the preferred style for many of the new churches built in Belfast (e.g. Duncairn, Fitzroy and Fortwilliam) and provincial towns and villages in the second half of the 1800s. The First Presbyterian (Non-Subscribing) Church in Newry is a particularly fine example of a Gothic Revival place of worship, as is the Cuningham Memorial Church in Cullybackey.

Not a few of these places of worship were the work of the famous architectural firm of Young & Mackenzie. This practice was also responsible for Assembly Buildings, the new headquarters of the Presbyterian Church in Ireland, which opened in 1905. It was designed in a rather mixed style, employing both Perpendicular Gothic and Scottish Baronial; the crown spire was designed in imitation of St Giles' Cathedral in Edinburgh. PRONI has an extensive collection of documents relating to Young & Mackenzie, including plans and specifications (D2194). A detailed study of the firm is provided by Paul Harron's book, *Architects of Ulster: Young & Mackenzie – A Transformational Provincial Practice 1850–1960* (2016), which includes a chapter devoted to ecclesiastical work. A further variety of architectural styles were on display in twentieth-century Presbyterian churches. A number of places of worship were built in the Art Nouveau style in the early 1900s, such as Hillhall, near Lisburn. In more recent decades a range of modern styles has been employed on new church buildings.

8.2 Title deeds

Many early Presbyterian meeting houses were built without any formal transfer of the site to the congregation by the landowner. For instance, there is no deed for the site of Bready Reformed Presbyterian Church in the townland of Tamnabrady, where Covenanters have been gathering for worship since the early 1770s. However, within the collection of records in PRONI relating to the management of the Abercorn estate, there are letters revealing how the site came into the possession of the congregation. On 6 June 1771 the 8th Earl of Abercorn – who, though a member of the Anglican establishment, had few qualms about granting sites for places of worship to those of a different religious persuasion – wrote to his land agent: 'I give my consent that the Covenanters may build a meeting house in Tavanabrady [Tamnabrady]' (D623/A/20/69). Just over a week later, on 14 June, the agent replied to the Earl on this matter: 'I let Mr James who is the minister to the Covenanters also know by a line, that your Lordship consents to their building a meeting house in Tavnabrady.' Building work probably began soon after this and an estate map, dating from 1777, marks the location of the meeting house (D623/D/1/16/5).

On other occasions, however, the site of the meeting house was conveyed to the congregation by a written deed. Typically, the deed includes the names of the minister and some of the members of the congregation acting as trustees. One of the earliest to survive is the deed issued by Arthur and Clotworthy Upton in 1693 conveying the new meeting house in Templepatrick and 24 feet of ground around it to Rev. Anthony Kennedy, the minister of the congregation (CR4/12/C/1). The Uptons were the landlords of Templepatrick and unusually among landowners were Presbyterians. They had their own 'aisle' in the meeting house and the terms of the deed included a clause protecting their access to it so long as they remained Presbyterians.

Copies of title deeds for the sites of Presbyterian meeting houses can also be found in the Registry of Deeds in Dublin.[5] In fact, the fourth and fifth deeds to be registered, on 15 April 1708, concern a Presbyterian place of worship in County Westmeath. A couple of further examples from the Registry of Deeds are presented here, the first concerning Strabane, the second Ballymena. On 9 July 1712 a deed was drawn up between, on the one hand, George McGhee and

Rebecca his wife, and on the other, John Love, John Wilson, David Bradley, Andrew Carson and Robert Askin, all merchants (book 10, page 161, no. 3309). Under the terms of this deed the site of the new meeting house in Strabane was conveyed to Love *et al.* by the McGhees. Very helpfully, the deed states that the previous meeting house had been on the west side of the Bowling Green in Strabane – the only known record of this.

Dating from 12 March 1744 [1745] is a deed from Sir Robert Adair conveying in fee farm (i.e. in perpetuity) the site of the Presbyterian meeting house and residence of the minister, Rev. John Brown, in the town of Ballymena to 15 representatives of the congregation (book 116, page 473, no. 81596). Those representing the congregation were: William Ker, merchant; David Philips and Alexander Adair, gentlemen; John Adair, David McKedy, William McKedy, Richard Lendrick, merchants; Robert Allen, apothecary; Alexander Young, wheelwright; John Gunnon, distiller (all of Ballymena); John Campbell of Ballygarvey; James Moore of Ballyreagh; Robert Philips of Dunclug; William Majore of Dunfane; and James Brown of Clinty. Since no congregational records exist before the nineteenth century this is a valuable record of the leading figures in the congregation around the middle of the eighteenth century.

A most unusual document in PRONI concerning a place of worship relates to Moira, County Down, and dates from 1790 (D1038/15). This is a deed of partition by which the Presbyterian and Secession congregations of Moira agreed to divide equally between them the meeting house and the acre of ground on which it stood. The parties to the deed were: Rev. David Trotter of Moira and James and Alexander Agnew of Tullyard, David Wilkie of Clare, William McCoy of Ballygowan, all in the parish of Moira, and William Brown of Kilmore, parish of Shankill, County Down, representing the Presbyterians; and Rev. Adam Gilbert of Ballymagaraghan, parish of Moira, and Robert McKeon, Harrymount, Hamilton Dobbin of Ballymagaraghan, Hugh Fulton of Ballymacbredan, William Hume of Ballykeel, and Samuel Lilburn of Gregorlough, all in the parish of Magheralin, County Down, representing the Seceders.

8.3 Records relating to the building and repair of meeting houses

Building or rebuilding a meeting house was a major financial and organisational undertaking on the part of a congregation and the decision to do so was not taken lightly. The need to build a meeting house could be for a number of different reasons. Most obviously it was when a new congregation was formed. Alternatively, a congregation may have outgrown its place of worship necessitating a new building. In some circumstances building a new meeting house made more sense than renovating the existing one. Occasionally, places of worship were destroyed either deliberately or accidentally. In 1743 Freeduff Presbyterian meeting house in County Armagh was burned in an arson attack.[6] In 1941 the Presbyterian church in York Street, Belfast, was one of a number of places of worship in the city destroyed as the result of German air raids.

Financing the work

For the most part, the funds required to build a Presbyterian meeting house were raised by the congregation itself. However, support from other quarters was also sought. For example, one of the principal supporters of the formation of the Third Presbyterian congregation in Belfast was Samuel Smith who travelled to Scotland in 1722 and 1723 to secure financial support for building the new meeting house. Using his business and Presbyterian contacts, he found support in many places. A positive response was received from the Provost and Corporation of Glasgow on the grounds that the new congregation would be following the doctrine of the Church of Scotland and that its members were of Scottish extraction. Others who provided support were the Lord Provost of Edinburgh, the Lord President of the Council, the Countess of Stair, Lady Dunmore, the Duke of Athol and the Earl of Buchan. These details of fundraising for the new Third Presbyterian meeting house in Belfast are recorded in the congregational accounts of the period (MIC1P/7/8).

As the section on congregational histories in Chapter 2 revealed, the inclusion of lists of subscribers towards building works is a common feature in these publications. The names of subscribers towards church building projects may also appear in the press. For example, a lengthy list of subscribers to the new First Derry meeting house was published in the *Londonderry Journal* on 16 January 1781. The names appearing in this list indicate that support came from outside the congregation, indeed outside of Presbyterianism. One of the largest contributions came from the Earl of Bristol, better known in that locality as the Anglican bishop of Derry, who donated £100.

Some subscription lists can be helpful in providing information on the members and adherents of other congregations. For instance, among the surviving records of the Reformed Presbyterian Church in Derry are lists of subscribers to the new meeting house from members of the Reformed Presbyterian congregations of Ballylaggan and Drimbolg in 1856 (CR5/13/4/1). In the case of Ballylaggan there are no records of the congregation in the public domain, while for Drimbolg there are no baptisms any earlier than 1895 (MIC1C/15).

Financial support was often sought from America and a number of ministers crossed the Atlantic on fundraising trips. In June 1843 Rev. Jonathan Simpson of Portrush set sail for North America, visiting 22 states of the United States as well as Canada and travelling some 7,000 miles in the process. The trip was successful and through it Simpson raised about £1,150 towards the costs of building a meeting house for his congregation. On several further visits to America he raised funds for additional congregational initiatives.[7] In September 1926 Rev. James Mark of First Dunboe left for the United States to raise money towards building a new meeting house. He took with him a fundraising brochure, which drew attention to the high levels of emigration from the congregation and the contribution of individuals and families to the US. 'We have given to America some of the very best of our people during the past 200 years', read the appeal, which went on to cite the exodus to New England in 1718 led by Rev. James Woodside of Dunboe, and the departure of another set of families from the congregation in 1839 to Pennsylvania.[8] Mark's six-month trip was a huge success, raising £3,600. Moreover, during his time in America the First Dunboe minister met two Crawford brothers, sons of a man from Castlerock, who initially gave £100 and then over the next 20 years contributed further donations to the congregation totalling more than £3,000.

Choosing a site

An obvious decision for the congregation, though one of the most contentious, was where to build the new meeting house. For existing congregations this was often straightforward – the new place of worship was built on the site of the old one. This was not always the case, however. The congregation of Urney was almost rent asunder in 1720s over a fractious dispute concerning the location of a new meeting house; the wrangling can be followed in the minutes of the Sub-Synod of Derry (CR3/46/3/1) and those of the Presbytery of Strabane (CR3/26/2/1). As noted above, the status of Presbyterians sometimes made it difficult to secure a site for their place of worship and they could not always be sure that a landowner would accede to their request. In the days when people walked to worship new congregations had to choose the best site for the majority of their members. This was no easy decision and some people on the geographical fringes were bound to be disappointed.

The difficulties for one congregation in securing a site for a meeting house can be explored through the pages of the minute book containing the proceedings of the committee of what was originally known as Cove Presbyterian Church (later Queenstown and later still Cobh) in County Cork (Cork City and County Archives, U100). This congregation was founded in the early 1840s. In 1842 Lord Midleton was approached for a site for a meeting house, but this was later deemed unsuitable. Subsequently, Mr Smith Barry offered a site, but this was withdrawn. In October 1848 the continued delay in finding a site was put down to 'private interests and unprincipled Agents and Architects'. There were further false starts in the early 1850s, before eventually, in October 1853, it was agreed to accept the offer of a site on Miss Rushbrooke's property. The construction of a place of worship began in 1854 and was completed the following year. The opening services were held on Sunday, 19 August 1855 when Rev. Dr Henry Cooke was the guest preacher.

Organising the work

One approach to building a meeting house was for the congregation to appoint a committee to oversee the work. This committee may have kept its own minutes of meetings and these can sometimes be found among congregational records. The way in which a building committee operated can be explored through the example of First Carrickfergus in the 1820s. Having reached the conclusion that a new meeting house was required for the expanding congregation, a building committee was formed in February 1826. Initially, the committee attempted to secure a better site for the meeting house and approached the local landlord, Lord Donegall, with a particular location in mind. Lord Donegall did not wish to grant them their preferred site, but was open to other suggestions. In the end, however, the meeting house was rebuilt on the existing site.

Preparations for building the new church took place over the course of the next year. One of the leading architects of his day, Thomas Duff, was commissioned to prepare plans for the building. The final service in the old meeting house was held on 1 April 1827, after which the building was demolished, though the materials were salvaged for use in constructing the new edifice. The foundation stone of the new church was laid on 9 May 1827. At this ceremony a bottle was placed in the foundation which contained a number of coins and a parchment recording the reasons for the new building and a list of names of the members of the building committee and the names of the principal workmen. The new meeting house was opened on Sunday, 8 February 1829.[9]

In addition to building committee minutes, there can also be accounts relating to the construction work, recording expenditure, such as payments for materials or to workmen. The building accounts for the new meeting house for the congregation of Kilbride, near Doagh, of 1848–50 provide a detailed record of the construction work and the different people involved.[10] To name some of them: the stonemason employed to carry out the building work was Samuel Courtney; John Creith was the plasterer; James Hull was responsible for the seating, the Communion table and the pulpit; the porch was built by Robert Hunter; Sam Clugston laid the flagstones in the porch and cut the caps for two pilasters; S. Todd roughcast the exterior of the building; the entrance gate was manufactured by David Boyd; A. Barr produced the door frames and other woodwork; the glazier was James Millar; Robert Marshall drew timber to the site; James Todd provided labour; Sam Clarke and James McConnell supplied sand; and among other actions Anthony Preston planted trees.

Few building contracts survive before the nineteenth century. One of the earliest is the agreement drawn up by the committee of

Kellswater Reformed Presbyterian Church with the masons, Robert Darragh of Tamnabrake and David Carnaghan of Shilvoden, on 16 July 1806 (CR5/9/7/2/1). The agreement specified the dimensions of the new meeting house – 62 feet by 36 feet with side walls 14 feet high – with further instructions on the windows, door frames, etc. The work was to be completed by 11 September 1806 with penalties for the late completion of the work or if it was judged inadequate. The building was duly completed and remains in use today. A stone built into the front wall of the meeting house names Darragh as the mason and also John Orr as the joiner. Agreements with contractors can also be found written into the pages of committee or Session minute books. For instance, the minutes of First Stewartstown include the following declaration by Adam McCambish:

> I agree to execute the flooring of 29 seats and the aisles of the First Presbyterian Church, Stewartstown. Sinking the floors 6 inches under the flooring and I hereby bind myself to finish all in a workmanlike manner or the sum of £3 8s. 0d., all materials being furnished by me.[11]

A small collection of documents in PRONI relating to the building of a new meeting house for Third Presbyterian Church in Belfast in the early 1830s includes a 17-page document detailing specifications for work to be undertaken (D3688/E). Architectural plans are available in some archives. The Young & Mackenzie archive in PRONI has already been mentioned. Other examples include photographic copies of original architectural plans and drawings of Trinity Presbyterian Church, Cork, from the 1860s in the Cork City and County Archives (SM688) and the plan and elevation for St Andrew's Presbyterian Church, Bray, County Wicklow, 1856, in the Irish Architectural Archive, Dublin (0092/046-0121-0122).

Before moving on from this section, it may be noted that many congregations had a separate Session-house – a detached building in the church grounds – which was the venue for meetings of the Session and other church bodies, such as the committee. Schools, both day schools and Sunday schools, were frequently held in Session-houses. For First Carrickfergus there is an account book which, among other things, contains a list of subscribers' names and subscriptions for building a Session-house, etc, 1815–16 (MIC1P/157/1). Stables were often constructed for the ease of worshippers arriving on horseback or in a horse-drawn carriage (or pony and trap). For example, a stable with eight stalls was built beside Clogher Presbyterian Church in 1833 for the exclusive use of the individuals who had contributed to the building costs.

8.4 Seating arrangements and records relating to them

The arrangement and allocation of the seating within Presbyterian meeting houses were at one time issues of some importance, providing a significant source of church funds and not infrequently giving rise to disputes that sometimes reached the higher courts of the Church. In the first instance, the Session or committee was responsible for seating arrangements in the meeting house. In 1647 the Session of Templepatrick ruled that 'the south syd of the church shall be for the seats of ye people of ye yond syd of ye watter, and ye north syd for this syd of the watter' – the 'watter' presumably being the Sixmilewater River.[12] The Session/committee allocated specific seating areas to the families of the congregation and set the fees for their occupancy. These fees were fixed annual sums payable at different times during the year. Known as pew rents, they generally went towards the minister's stipend; this practice survived in most churches into the twentieth century. On other occasions, especially when a new meeting house was constructed, the Session/committee 'sold' seats to members (see below for more on this).

The approach adopted with regard to seats and the fees charged for them varied considerably from congregation to congregation and much about this subject area remains uncertain. Even Rev. T. H. Mullin, whose knowledge of Presbyterian history was second to none, was forced to admit, 'I am not quite clear as to how this system operated', when discussing the purchase of seats in Aghadowey meeting house.[13] Various rights and privileges accrued to the possession of a seat. For example, access to the ceremonies of baptism and marriage was often linked to having a seat in the meeting house. In 1809 the Session of First Dunboe ruled that those 'who can only say they belong to this congregation, but who do not hold seats and are very irregular in their attendance at public worship' would have to have their conduct examined by Session before their children would be baptised.[14]

To a certain extent, where people sat during public worship was a reflection of their personal circumstances and status in society. Those who could pay more were allocated seats in what were considered the best positions. Unsurprisingly, this could cause considerable ructions. Rev. John Kennedy of Benburb recorded in his diary under 7 June 1727, 'Met about seats at meeting house[;] did little good and saw pride and folly'.[15] In some congregations there were different classes of pew-sitters. For example, in the early nineteenth century pew-sitters in Glendermott Presbyterian Church were divided into gentlemen, farmers, and artisans/cottiers, who paid the following pew rents, respectively, £1 10s., £1 and 15s.[16]

Once granted, the possession of a seating area in the meeting house was guarded carefully and, to quote Professor Barkley, a 'sort of "tenant right"' developed.[17] Many rows over seats concerned complaints that some people had 'intruded' into seating areas reserved for others. In 1771 the committee of First Presbyterian Church, Belfast went so far as to have locks placed on the doors of unoccupied seats with the keys kept in the vestry. There was often a battle between the Session/committee and individuals within the membership over seating rights. In 1703 a Mrs Boyd was cited by the Aghadowey Session for, among other things, 'fencing in her seat', thus preventing anyone else from using it while she, for a time, abandoned the congregation for the Established Church.

If disputes over seating arrangements could not be settled at congregational level they were referred to the relevant presbytery (see Chapter 6 for more on presbytery records). In October 1815 James Donnel, a member of the Carrickfergus congregation, appeared before Presbytery of Templepatrick complaining that 'Robt Lockhart, Thos Hagan, James Millar and Robt McIlwrath had deprived him of his seat in their Meeting House'. The Presbytery ruled that Donnel should be 'restored to that share of the seat his grandfather had enjoyed, and that he be enjoined to bring no person with him to the seat in future ... he having failed in proving his title to that share his uncle held of that seat.' The Presbytery urged the Carrickfergus committee to give 'more attention to private rights' in dealing with cases like this.[18]

The actual appearance of the seating in earlier times is a matter of some conjecture. In Templepatrick in 1647 it was agreed that 'Session are to pew the whole church everie pew being one syse'.[19] Stories have been handed down of the simplicity of the seats in the earliest meeting houses, perhaps nothing more than logs.[20] It also seems to have been the case that seats were constructed by the worshippers themselves, at least by those who could afford to do so. In these situations there was inevitably some disparity in the form of the seating in a meeting house. Later more uniform pews became standard. However, differences in the seating continued due to members of their own volition making alterations and repairs to their seats. In the 1770s one member of First Belfast spent the considerable sum of six guineas repairing his seat.

In a number of instances the Session/committee was forced to intervene in disputes over the form of the seats. In 1825 the Carrickfergus committee heard complaints that some people 'under pretence of improving their seats [had] altered and raised them to the inconvenience of the neighbouring seatholders'; in response the committee ruled that no alterations to the seats should be made without permission.[21] In the rules drawn up for seat-holders in the new Presbyterian meeting house in May Street, Belfast, there was a stipulation that no alterations were to be made to the pews with the exception of cushions and linings and these were to be of the same colour as the drapery of the pulpit. When Rev. R. B. Wylie became minister of Terrace Row, Coleraine, in 1871 he found the pews to be 'very uncomfortable and most unsightly', with high, straight backs. As a result, 'Only the heads of the older people were visible from the pulpit, while the children were lost'. In addition, many of the pews were painted in a range of different colours. It was therefore agreed that to 'cut down and lean back the pews' and paint them uniformly.[22]

In 1820 the Millisle congregation revised its rules concerning seating arrangements in the meeting house. This had been prompted by situations where seat-holders had 'sublet' to others or parents had subdivided their sittings with their children, giving rise to a rather confused state of affairs and a lack of clarity on who was paying what and to whom. In summary, the new regulations stated that: 'there shall be no under sitters' and that applications for seats should be made to the committee alone; after a certain period of time those who fell into arrears would forfeit their seats; those who married were expected to take a seat for themselves and no longer sit with their parents; persons who could not afford to pay would be allocated seats in the meeting house free of charge on making their situation known to the Session and committee. Space remained at a premium, however, resulting in a further regulation that only two members of each family or household would be permitted to attend the Sunday service.[23]

Those who fell behind in their payments were liable to censure. In Second Ballymena the congregation adopted several measures to try to ensure that pew rents were paid: a resolution of 1832 was to post notices on the seats of those who were in arrears with the threat that if they did not pay up their seats would be disposed of; in 1836 it was agreed that those who owed more than a year's stipend would be prosecuted through the civil courts; and in 1838 the decision was taken at the AGM to read out in public the names of those in arrears.[24]

The Session/committee reserved the right to allocate particular areas for specific groups of people. For example, in the new meeting house built in Rosemary Street in Belfast in the early 1720s – the place of worship of Third Presbyterian Church – three pews in the gallery were set aside for the exclusive use of visiting merchants and mariners from Scotland; this was in recognition of the financial support provided by Scots towards the building work. The provision of seating for the poor can also be found in the rules drawn up for the new place of worship in May Street, Belfast, where the minister was authorised to loan money to the poor of the congregation to allow them to pay their stipend; the minister would then be reimbursed by the committee without having to name those to whom he had provided funds.[25]

The sale of seats often followed the construction of a new meeting house and was one way of clearing the building debt. According to the historian of Third Presbyterian Church, Belfast, 'Very substantial amounts were received from the sale of pews to individual proprietors' following the completion of the new meeting house in 1726.[26] In this congregation, as elsewhere, seats became a tradable commodity, which their possessors could bequeath, sublet or even sell. The Session and committee, however, reserved the right to approve the sale of a seat and a record of the sales and transfers of seats was maintained; documentary proof of the right to occupy a pew was also required before a conveyance could take place. In 1749 a seat in Third Presbyterian Church, which had formerly been occupied by Samuel Smith, was sold to John Potts and Thomas Greg for £11 (D298/16; see also D298/20, /21). Following the death of John Hunter of Greenhill, Aghadowey, his house and farm were advertised for sale in the *Coleraine Chronicle* of 10 March 1849. Included in the sale was 'a Double-Seated PEW, in the Aughadoey Presbyterian Meeting-House, with Cushions, Lining &c., complete.'

The fact that the members of a congregation were able to purchase their seats did not excuse them from paying pew rents. In the recently opened Second Ballymena Presbyterian Church, the forerunner of today's Wellington congregation, a list of seat-holders was drawn up in August 1829, which included the following preamble:

> We the undersigned purchasers and proprietors of seats in the Meeting House of the Second Presbyterian Congregation in Ballymena, do hereby engage to pay in addition to the purchase money of our seats the sum of stipend assessed upon said seats by the present committee.[27]

The rules drawn up for the new congregation in May Street, Belfast, in 1829 included the form of the certificate to be issued to purchasers of pews:

> This debenture witnesseth that _____ has paid £__ in said church, subject to the annual stipend rent of £__, and subject to such rules as are now or hereafter may be made for the management of said church.

The May Street rules allowed the purchasers of pews to dispose of them by will or by sale, though in the case of the latter they were to first offer the pew to the committee at the original purchase price.[28]

The records generated by the regulation of the seating arrangements provide a rich source of information on individuals and families and an insight into the issues at stake. As the above examples indicate, there is much to be found about seating arrangements in the minutes of Session and presbytery meetings. In addition, there can be congregational records recording the sales of seats and the setting and collection of pew rents. For Third Belfast there is a record of the sales of seats in the new meeting house in 1726, which provides the names of the purchasers and the amounts paid (T654/6). In his history of Millisle and Ballycopeland, Thomas Kilpatrick reproduces a document titled, '19th August, 1776. Sittings let by the Committee to members of the congregation [of Millisle], together with the amounts of Stipend paid quarterly'.[29] The occupants of 37 pews are listed, some of whom paid for more than one sitting; Adam Gonnan in pew 26 had four sittings. Pew rent books can be particularly interesting documents and can provide clues to when a member died or a family emigrated.

8.5 Places of burial for Presbyterians

Many Presbyterian meeting houses, particularly in rural settings (at least when they were founded), have an adjoining burial ground. However, judging by the dates on gravestones, the practice of burying within the grounds of a Presbyterian place of worship does not seem to have occurred until the mid eighteenth century at the earliest. In fact, most graveyards adjoining a Presbyterian place of worship date from no earlier than the 1800s.[30] Before this, and indeed for long afterwards, Presbyterians buried their dead in the parish churchyard or in an ancient burial ground attached to a disused monastery. The absence of early Presbyterian graveyards was, at least in part, an outworking of the discrimination that Presbyterians faced as a result of the Penal Laws. The only burial service permitted was one conducted by an Anglican clergyman and appropriate fees had to be paid to that clergyman for the burial service. There were, of course, attempts to get around this and not just by Presbyterians. In explaining the low number of entries in the Donagheady burial register for 1754 and 1755, the rector, Rev. George Bracegirdle, wrote:

> The reason so few burials are entered is an indecent custom of interring without sending to the minister to attend. That the papists should always and the Presbyterians generally omit is not to be wondered; but it is astonishing that those who are of the established church should choose to bury their deceased friends like dogs (MIC1/35).

In one notorious incident in the parish of Loughgilly, County Armagh, in the mid 1700s the Church of Ireland rector had the body of a Presbyterian, whose family had not paid the burial fee, exhumed. It was left decomposing on the ground until local people had it buried again and drove the rector from his parish.[31] Even after burial grounds began to be laid out around Presbyterian meeting houses, the practice of interment in older graveyards continued for many families. When Rev. Robert Magill of Antrim died in 1839 he was buried in not one but two old graveyards. Initially, at the direction of his second wife, his earthly remains were laid to rest in Templepatrick. However, his body was later exhumed and interred in the parish churchyard in Donegore where his first wife and son were buried.

There were a number of incidents in the nineteenth century that had an impact on the use by Presbyterians of graveyards in the legal ownership of the Church of Ireland. An episode in Greyabbey is highlighted below. The background to the opening of Balmoral Cemetery in 1855 was an incident in which a Church of Ireland minister obstructed a funeral being conducted by two Presbyterian ministers. One of the ministers involved, Rev. Joseph Mackenzie, secured the ground for the cemetery, which was managed by a board of trustees. Though the cemetery was never exclusively Presbyterian, it was predominantly so and was the only burial place of its kind in nineteenth-century Ireland. Many of Belfast's leading Presbyterians during the Victorian period were buried here, including the most high profile Presbyterian of his day, Rev. Dr Henry Cooke; one of the first missionaries sent by the Presbyterian Church to India, Rev. James Glasgow; and one of the moving forces in the formation of the Presbyterian Orphan Society, Dr Wilberforce Arnold. PRONI holds the register of the cemetery, 1855–96 (D1075/6) and also a notebook of burials, 1908–11 (D2966/64/1). In 1953 the cemetery was taken over by Belfast Corporation (now Belfast City Council).[32]

8.6 Presbyterian burial grounds

The graveyards adjoining Presbyterian meeting houses are generally in good condition and well maintained. One of the oldest is the graveyard at the former Non-Subscribing Presbyterian Church in Antrim, where there are several memorials from the late 1700s. These include the headstone to William Eckles, a Presbyterian weaver resident in Scotch Quarter, who was killed during the Battle of Antrim in June 1798. It is said that some others killed in the battle were buried here surreptitiously, in graves dug quietly at night and without coffins.[33] At the lower end of the burial ground at First Saintfield there are two headstones to men from Killinchy who died at the Battle of Saintfield in 1798; in more recent times this area has been turned into a Memorial Garden.

In the first half of the nineteenth century there are many examples of the conversion of the 'meeting house green', as it was often called, to a burial ground. At a congregational meeting on 5 November 1826 the members of First Dunboe decided to allow interments within the grounds of their place of worship. Henceforth, the members of the congregation were 'at liberty to bury their dead in the Meeting House Yard', subject to the following conditions: 'the Meeting House Yard be not disfigured by carrying earth from one place to another to make up graves'; and 'all persons submit to a committee, now to be appointed, the place and manner of burial'. No fewer than 50 people were nominated to serve on the graveyard committee. However, not everyone was happy with this. In the words of a later minister:

> The youth of the village of Articlave evidently resented the idea of turning what had been regarded as a village park and common into a burying-ground, and when the first interment was made in it, they threatened to raise the corpse.[34]

Burying their dead beside the meeting house was slow to catch on and nearly a decade later there were still only 15 graves and one tombstone in the grounds of First Dunboe.

Even though there may be no burial ground at the current meeting house, it is worth checking to see if there is an older site which does have a place of interment. For example, there is no graveyard at Benburb Presbyterian Church, though there is one at the site of its predecessor at Lisduff. The local landlord, Lord Powerscourt, agreed to cover the cost of constructing a wall around this burial ground and in 1844 John Archer was paid £57 6s. 2d. for doing so; for building materials Archer used the stones from the old meeting house.[35]

Millisle Presbyterian Church was founded in the early 1770s, but the first person to be buried in the portion of ground adjoining the meeting house was Rev. John Hanna, the pastor of the congregation, who died in 1850. The congregation's historian, Rev. Thomas

Kilpatrick, wrote lyrically about the burial ground and its importance to the members of the congregation:

> God's House was now surrounded by God's-Acre, a place of solemn and sorrowful memories for many a member of Millisle. … Many a sorrowful company has wended its way to the churchyard at Millisle, and many a heart has been empty because a grave has been filled. But the sorry ones have grieved not as those who have no hope. The Church beside their beloved dead has proclaimed its message of comfort and of strength. … A place very sad yet very dear to the members of Old Millisle is thus their little sea-girt churchyard.[36]

Some new congregations established in the nineteenth century made provision for a burial ground from the outset. The present Downpatrick Presbyterian Church came into existence in the mid 1820s and a meeting house was built in 1826–7. A gravestone in the adjoining burial ground records the death in 1828 of Robert Thompson Young 'whose body was the first interred in this ground'. On the other hand, a congregation might have been in existence for quite a few years before a place of interment was laid out. Claggan Presbyterian Church, founded in 1846, did not have a graveyard of its own for the first two decades of its existence. In February 1866 a daughter of George Ramsay of Claggan House, whose family had been instrumental in the formation of the congregation, died in infancy. Ramsay wanted his child to be buried near the meeting house and chose a site on his own property overlooking the building. Following her interment, Ramsay and the members of Claggan came to a mutual agreement that a congregational burial ground should be established here also. The site was transferred into the possession of the congregation in 1867, trustees were appointed, and the graveyard was divided into about 100 burial plots. These were sold to the members of the congregation for five shillings; the money raised was used to build the graveyard wall.[37]

Generally speaking, congregations have been careful to restrict burial rights only, or at least primarily, to members and contributors to church funds. In 1840 the committee of Magherally resolved that only stipend payers could be buried in the congregation's cemetery. In October 1837 the grounds around the recently opened meeting house at Malone, Belfast, were advertised for burial plots, though for the first three months priority was given to members of the congregation; in 1862, when burial space was becoming scarce, graves were restricted to seat-holders.[38]

8.7 Records relating to graveyards and burials

As the abovementioned example of Dunboe indicates, some congregations established a graveyard committee with specific responsibility for the maintenance and regulation of the burial ground. Minute books of the graveyard committee can occasionally be found among congregational records. For example, there is a 'Graveyard Book' for Killinchy Non-Subscribing Presbyterian Church, which includes the rules of the burial ground, the minutes of the meetings of the graveyard committee (c. 1874–1882), and the names of persons buried (CR4/17/C/1). The formation of such a committee may have been in response to a particular set of circumstances. In 1935 a graveyard committee was formed in Drumreagh in an attempt to deal with disputes that were arising over claims to burial plots. In addition, the sexton of Drumreagh was requested to keep goats and hens out of the graveyard and the gravedigger was asked to ensure that there should be at least four feet between the top of the coffin and the level of the ground.[39]

In the 1850s there was a major dispute in Greyabbey over the rights of Presbyterians to bury in the graveyard adjoining the ruins of the former Cistercian abbey. The Anglican incumbent, with the support of the local landowner, decided to enclose the area used by Presbyterians and to levy taxes on further burials and the erecting of headstones. This provoked a massive outcry and a committee was formed to defend Presbyterian burial rights. In June 1857 three men, one of whom was the Presbyterian minister, Rev. David Jeffrey, were charged by the Church of Ireland authorities with 'brawling in church', causing even greater outrage among Presbyterians.[40]

Presumably created in connection with the episode, PRONI has an 1857 map of the graveyard with a key to burials (T1619). PRONI also has an interesting document in the form of a minute book of the 'Greyabbey Graveyard Committee at the First Presbyterian Meetinghouse', recording details of a memorial to the Lord Lieutenant seeking access to the burial ground, improvements to the graveyard, and a petty sessions court case relating to 'interfering with the trees' at the graveyard, 1872–93 (D3815/D/2).

Other documents relating to burial grounds can be found in the archives. PRONI has a set of documents relating to a court case in July 1910 concerning an alleged obstruction of a right-of-way through the meeting house gate of Killymurris Presbyterian Church for the purpose of erecting a tombstone (D2792/2/1). The material generated by the case includes submissions by members of the congregational graveyard committee and are revealing of the practices associated with a burial ground adjoining a Presbyterian place of worship.[41] Some graveyard maps and plans are available. For example, PRONI has maps of the graveyard adjoining Castlereagh Presbyterian Church of 1889 and 1947 (MIC1P/431), and a plan prepared in 1974 of the graveyard at Killinchy Non-Subscribing Presbyterian Church, showing names of persons buried in each plot (CR4/17/J/1). The Reside Archive in Newry & Mourne Museum, a collection created by Major G. W. Reside, an architect and engineer based in Newry, includes a number of twentieth-century plans of Presbyterian graveyards in south Armagh and south Down. Other records of this nature remain in local custody.

There are relatively few early burial registers among congregational records. Those burial registers – or sometimes simply death registers – that do exist generally begin in the late nineteenth century or even the early twentieth century. The information recorded can include the name of the deceased, the date of death and/or burial and occasionally the occupation and age at death. The cause of death was also recorded in some registers, as was the place of burial, and occasionally some remarks on the character of the deceased. One very interesting early eighteenth-century document relating to the burial of Presbyterians survives among the records of First Presbyterian Church in Belfast. It is a record of the hiring out of funeral gear – palls, cloaks and hats – for about 2,000 funerals which took place between 1712 and 1736. Though the funeral gear was hired in Belfast, the actual funerals took place over a wide area. This document has been published as *Funeral Register of Rosemary Street Non-Subscribing Presbyterian Church (known as the First Presbyterian Church of Belfast), 1712–36*, edited by Jean Agnew (Ulster Historical Foundation, 1995).

8.8 Memorials and inscriptions

For the most part, the inscriptions on headstones erected by Presbyterians do not differ a great deal from memorials erected by adherents of other denominations. Depending on the level of detail, dates of death, family relationships, places of residence can all be recorded on their memorials. Quotations from the Bible recur with some frequency. Gravestones to ministers might include some details on their pastorates, such as where and for how long they had served, and their characteristics. The inscription on the memorial to Rev. Sinclair Kelburn in the graveyard at Castlereagh Presbyterian Church reads:

> Here rests in hope of a resurrection in everlasting life, all that is earthly of the Revd Sinclair Kelburn who for 22 years, with much propriety and piety, sustained the character of Dissenting Minister of 3rd Congregation in Belfast. Obiit 31st of March 1802, aged 48 years. This monument was erected to his memory Anno Domini MDCCCXII by his relict Frances Kelburn.

Occasionally a gravestone inscription will draw attention to an individual's role in his local congregation. In the burial ground adjoining Ballygowan Presbyterian Church there is a gravestone to Arthur Alexander, who died in 1843, which was erected by his daughter Grace and which tells us that, 'He was long ruling elder in the Presbyterian Church, first at Saintfield and afterwards at Ballygowan'. A memorial in Banbridge reads: 'Erected by the members of Scarva Street Presbyterian Church in memory of William John Brady, late of Tullyear who for many years faithfully served the congregation as precentor, ruling elder and Sabbath school teacher. He died on 26th June 1891 aged 53 years.' A memorial at Bailiesmills Reformed Presbyterian Church to William Graham of Creevy, who died in 1828 in his 83rd year, is forthright in proclaiming the deceased's devotion to Covenanting principles:

> The following sentences written by himself are inscribed at his own request ... I testify against all who deal falsely in the cause of Christ – all who own the Covenants National and Solemn League and yet swear allegiance to the support of Prelacy ... I testify against all opposers of the Covenanted Cause, all who have departed from

Reformation and die giving my full approbation of that cause for which the martyrs suffered and which they sealed with their blood.

In the early eighteenth century the inscription placed on the tombstone of a Presbyterian minister was so controversial that it reached the highest court of the Church. The minister was Rev. Joshua Fisher of Donaghmore, County Donegal, who died in 1706, and the inscription had been composed by his son Hugh who was preparing to follow his father into the ministry. The people of Donaghmore took offence at something that had been written and caused such a ruckus that the Presbytery of Convoy refused to license Hugh. The young man then took his case to the Synod of Ulster in 1707 arguing that it would be 'a Dash on his Father's memory to raze the inscription'. The Synod did not order Hugh to remove the offensive part, but rebuked him for having acted unwisely; the people of Donaghmore were urged to 'surcease any heat in the matter'.[42]

A degree of caution should be exercised with regard to the accuracy of the details recorded on a gravestone. For example, the headstone in Racavan graveyard, County Antrim, erected in memory of Rev. David Park, formerly of Buckna Presbyterian Church, records his date of death as 15 January 1820. However, the minutes of the General Synod of Ulster state that he died on 10 March 1814. The headstone in Racavan was erected by Park's great-grandson. Even in death ministers could suffer a degree of ignominy. In his history of Convoy, Mullin relates how the gravestone of Rev. Robert Law (d. 1793) in the burial ground adjoining Convoy Presbyterian Church, was used by a local woman to 'beetle' her clothes and eventually was broken.[43]

Memorials and monuments can also be found within Presbyterian places of worship. Usually these commemorate a former minister or an individual whose family was prominent in the congregation. Larne and Kilwaughter Non-Subscribing Presbyterian Church (also known as the 'Old Presbyterian Church') has a very interesting collection of memorials. A mural tablet in the vestibule, bordered by 16 five-pointed stars and a rope, with a crown and anchor above, was erected by Daniel McNeale Beatty, commander in the Royal Navy, in memory of his wife of 45 years, Jane Stewart, who died in 1874. Other monuments commemorate individuals who died in Rio de Janeiro, in the Bay of Bengal off Ceylon (Sri Lanka), and in

Demerara (now British Guiana), South America. Nearly every Presbyterian congregation will have at least one war memorial, usually inside the meeting house, but occasionally in the church grounds. There may be separate memorials for the First and Second World Wars, or there might be a single memorial for both conflicts. Sometimes the memorial will name those who were killed, though many also record those who served and survived.[44]

8.9 Published inscriptions

The inscriptions from many Presbyterian burial grounds have been published in one form or another. An early example is the article titled, 'On the Tombstones of the Early Presbyterian Ministers of Ireland', which was published in the *Belfast Magazine and Literary Journal*, vol. 1, no. 4 (May 1825), pp 351–5. The Ulster Historical Foundation has published the inscriptions from more than 50 Presbyterian graveyards in County Down as well as several more in County Antrim in its *Gravestone Inscriptions Series*. A number of local historical societies and other bodies have also been involved in transcribing and publishing gravestone inscriptions. The *Ballymena Borough Gravestone Series* of the 1990s featured several Presbyterian graveyards in Mid Antrim, including those adjoining Kellswater Reformed Presbyterian Church, First and Second Killymurris, and the Old Methodist Church in Cullybackey (which was originally the place of worship of a Secession congregation).

Congregational histories sometimes include gravestone inscriptions. Leslie McKeague has written two detailed books on congregations past and present in east County Cavan: *Trinity Presbyterian Church Bailieborough: The First 125 Years 1887–2012 (Incorporates the Churches of 2nd Bailieborough and Seafin)* (2013); and *First Bailieborough Presbyterian Church (Corglass): 300 Years of Worship 1714–2014 (Incorporates Glasleck Presbyterian Church, Shercock* (2014). The *Trinity Presbyterian Church* volume includes the inscriptions from Urcher Old graveyard (the location of Second Bailieborough, the forerunner of Trinity Bailieborough) and Urcher New graveyard, as well as maps of both burial grounds showing the location of the memorials; this volume also includes a list of the inscriptions in the graveyard of the former congregation of Seafin and a map of the burial ground. Likewise, his book on *First Bailieborough* includes inscriptions from and a map of the burial ground adjoining that place of worship and the same for the graveyard at the now closed Glasleck Presbyterian Church (in this case the map of the graveyard dates from 1941, with additional information added concerning memorials erected since then).

Collections of inscriptions made by genealogists and antiquarians can also be found in archives and libraries in Ireland. Rev. George Jackson, minister of Glenarm and Cairnalbana from 1931 to 1970, was a keen local historian and genealogist and copies of some of his papers and compilations are in PRONI (T3054). These include gravestone inscriptions from a number of burial grounds in the district in which he ministered, including Glenarm 'Old Meetinghouse Green burying ground' (the Non-Subscribing Presbyterian Church) and Buckna Presbyterian Church, near Broughshane. For each of these graveyards there is an alphabetical index to the names of memorials and a plan of the burial ground. PRONI also holds the extensive McClay collection of inscriptions from many graveyards (including Presbyterian burial grounds) in counties Antrim and Londonderry (D3672).

Increasingly, gravestone inscriptions are being made available online through various providers. Using an Internet search engine it ought to be possible to discover if the inscriptions from a graveyard have been transcribed and placed online. The inscriptions recorded by some of the genealogy centres affiliated to the Irish Family History Foundation are available through RootsIreland (www.rootsireland.ie). The county source lists in John Grenham's *Tracing Your Irish Ancestors* (5th edition, 2019) include details of the availability of many collections of gravestone inscriptions, especially those published in local journals as well as online.

Notes

[1] Thomas Mellon, *Thomas Mellon and His Times* (1994), p. 302. A replica of this meeting house is in the Ulster American Folk Park, close to the cottage in which Thomas Mellon was born in 1813. In 1818 Mellon emigrated to America, where he became a successful businessman and prominent judge.

2 J. Carroll, 'The excavation of the Old Presbyterian Meetinghouse at Ramelton, Co. Donegal', *Archaeology Ireland*, 3:2 (Summer, 1989), pp 61–3.

3 Information on architects and their works has been collated by the Irish Architectural Archive through its Dictionary of Irish Architects project and made available online (www.dia.ie).

4 The pedimented front was replaced in 1833, while the original Venetian window at the east end was removed in the early 1900s.

5 The Registry of Deeds was established by an act passed in the Irish Parliament in 1707. The aim of the act was to provide one central office in Dublin 'for the public registering of all deeds, conveyances and wills that shall be made of any honours, manors, lands, tenements or hereditaments'. The Registry of Deeds opened in 1708 and contains copies of deeds from across Ireland until the partition of the island in the early 1920s. The Registry of Deeds is located in Henrietta Street (the main entrance faces on to Constitution Hill) and is open to the public free of charge. Transcriptions of the registered deeds can now be viewed on the FamilySearch website.

6 See depositions relating to this incident in PRONI: T1392/1; T808/14925.

7 W. D. Killen, *History of Congregations of the Presbyterian Church in Ireland* (1886), pp 218–19.

8 The brochure is reproduced in McCaughan, *Dunboe*, p. 38.

9 McCartney, *Carrickfergus*, pp 188–94.

10 *Kilbride*, pp 91–7.

11 *On the Steps of the Meeting House ... Stewartstown*, p. 20.

12 W. T. Latimer, 'The old session-book of Templepatrick Presbyterian Church', *JRSAI*, 5th series, vol. 11 (1901), p. 264.

13 Mullin, *Aghadowey*, p. 161.

14 McCaughan, *Dunboe*, p. 69.

15 Bailie, *Benburb*, p. 6.

16 *Ordnance Survey Memoirs of Ireland Vol. 34: Parishes of County Londonderry XIII: Clondermot and the Waterside* (1996), p. 24.

17 Barkley, *Short History of the Presbyterian Church in Ireland*, p. 102.

18 McCartney, *Carrickfergus*, p. 167.

19 Latimer, The old session-book of Templepatrick', p. 264.

20 Mark, *First Dunboe*, p. 10.

21 McCartney, *Carrickfergus*, p. 185.

22 Wylie, *Terrace Row ... Coleraine*, p. 58.

23 Kilpatrick, *Millisle*, p. 29.

24 Leith, *Wellington Street ... Ballymena*, p. 60.

25 Williamson, *May Street ... Belfast*, p. 19.

[26] Kernohan, *Rosemary Street … Belfast*, p. 15.

[27] Leith, *Wellington Street … Ballymena*, p. 59.

[28] Williamson, *May Street*, pp 19–20.

[29] Kilpatrick, *Millisle*, pp 9–13.

[30] An apparent exception is the graveyard to the rear of Drumbo Presbyterian Church, which includes memorials from the late seventeenth century. In this case, however, the meeting house was built next to the site of a medieval parish church; in other words, the graveyard was there long before the meeting house. Similarly Kilbride Presbyterian Church stands next to a graveyard going back to pre-Reformation times.

[31] Kevin Whelan, *Religion, Landscape and Settlement in Ireland* (2018), p. 85.

[32] The inscriptions are published in vol. 3 of the Ulster Historical Foundation's gravestone inscriptions series for Belfast. See also Tom Hartley, *Balmoral Cemetery* (2019).

[33] W. S. Smith, 'Memories of '98', *UJA*, 2nd series, vol. 1 (Jan. 1895), p. 138.

[34] Mark, *First Dunboe*, p. 25.

[35] Bailie, *Benburb*, p. 9.

[36] Kilpatrick, *Millisle*, pp 39–41.

[37] Kilpatrick, *Claggan*, pp 18–19.

[38] Robb, *Malone*, p. 31.

[39] Blair, *Drumreagh*, pp 79–80.

[40] See John T. Carson, 'The Greyabbey Brawling Case', *BPHSI*, vol. 4 (1974), pp 10–16.

[41] The case can be followed in the *Northern Whig* of 22 and 25 July 1910.

[42] A. G. Lecky, *Roots of Presbyterianism in Donegal* (1978), p. 65.

[43] Mullin, *Convoy*, p. 132.

[44] For a study of the people from one Presbyterian congregation who served in the First World War, see Fiona Berry, *Names Carved in Stone: The Stories of Some of Those Individuals Who Once Attended the Mall Presbyterian Church, Armagh Before They Marched Off to the Great War* (2016).

9

Presbyterian publications

9.1 Presbyterians and the printed word

In the second half of the seventeenth century Presbyterians in Ireland began to use the printed word to advance their cause or defend themselves from attacks by their opponents. An early example is the publication by the minister of Cookstown, Rev. John Mackenzie, *Narrative of the Siege of Londonderry* (1690), which was produced in response to an account of the siege by Rev. George Walker, a Church of Ireland minister, which had downplayed significantly the role of Presbyterians in defending the city. In the 1690s a series of publications by Rev. Joseph Boyse of Dublin and Rev. Robert Craghead of Donaghmore (County Donegal) defended Presbyterians from William King, the Anglican bishop of Derry. Of benefit to Presbyterians in particular was the founding in Belfast in the mid 1690s of the first commercial printing press known to have operated in the north of Ireland; the printers were Patrick Neill and James Blow, the former from Glasgow and the latter possibly from Culross in Fife. Other printing firms were established in the following decades. Much of their output was aimed at the local Presbyterian community with many books and pamphlets dealing with religious controversies (especially the subscription debate) or the relationship between Presbyterians and the state.

While many of these books are taken up with complex theological arguments, occasionally information of human interest will be found in them. A good example of an early eighteenth-century book by an Irish Presbyterian minister is *An Historical Essay upon the Loyalty of Presbyterians in Great Britain and Ireland ...* (1713) by Rev. James Kirkpatrick of Belfast. The following paragraph from it reproduces a portion of a certificate prepared by a Presbyterian who had refused to have his new-born child baptised by the Church of Ireland minister of Knockbreda parish, County Down:

> I James Moor of Castle reagh solemnly declare that about June the 10th 1711 my wife was delivered of a very weak Child six or eight Weeks before her time, and that I was urg'd by Mrs Woods and Jane Stanhouse to have it baptized by Mr Finnyston, then keeping Court in Mr Wood's House, but my self, and seeing John Montgomery (Who is no Elder) pass by the Road, I went out and ask'd his Opinion, and found it the same with my own Judgment, and spoke to no man else, and the Child died within three hours after it was born, and I buried it at Knock that Evening (p. 561).

Many older publications can now be accessed for free online through the Internet Archive (archive.org), Google Books and HathiTrust. A fascinating compendium of writings by Presbyterian ministers is found in Thomas Witherow, *Historical and Literary Memorials of Presbyterianism in Ireland*, published in two volumes in 1879–80, the first covering the period 1623–1731 and the second 1731–1800. For each of his writers Witherow listed their publications, provided biographical details, and included excerpts from one or more of their works, many of them obscure and little known. The Antrim Presbytery Collection in Special Collections at Queen's University Belfast comprises literary, philosophical and theological volumes mainly published before 1800 that were acquired by non-subscribing congregations in Belfast and Antrim. Not all of the books were written by Presbyterians, but the collection provides an insight into the range of material being read by the ministers of these churches.

9.2 Presbyterian magazines

In the period 1829–32 each of the four major groups of Presbyterians in Ireland began to publish a magazine of their own: *The Orthodox Presbyterian* was published by the Synod of Ulster; *The Bible Christian* by the Non-Subscribers; *The Christian Freeman* by the Seceders; and *The Covenanter* by the Reformed Presbyterians. These periodicals included a mix of news and comment on current affairs with articles of a devotional and historical nature. Trenchant views were often expressed on the activities and theological positions of other denominations. Most of these publications had ceased by the mid 1840s. *The Christian Freeman* seems to have only appeared between 1832 and 1836. However, *The Covenanter*, though there is a gap 1848–52, is still being published today as *The Covenanter Witness*. For more on these early publications and some others that appeared at this time, see the article by Rev. Prof. J. M. Barkley, 'Irish Presbyterian Magazines, 1829–1840' in the first issue of the *BPHSI* (1970), which is available to read for free on the PHSI website. Barkley also contributed articles to the *BPHSI* on 'Irish Non-Subscribing Magazines 1830–1883' (1972) and 'Irish Presbyterian Magazines, 1840–1974' (1974).

From a genealogical perspective these periodicals usefully include personal announcements, especially obituaries and death notices. For example, the following information is abbreviated from the Obituary section of *The Bible Christian* of January 1838 (p. 431):

Died on Friday, 21st ult. [December], near Holywood, Thomas Byers in the 79th year of his age; an elder in the First Presbyterian Congregation of Holywood.

Died on 10th ult. [December], at the house of his father, Holywood, Captain Hugh Stewart, only surviving son of Mr Hugh Stewart, in his 23rd year; for some time he had been at sea and had visited the East Indies, South America and other countries.

Died on 4 December, at his house in George's Street, Belfast, James Harper, aged 50.

Died on 4 December, John Cunningham, aged 25.

Through its website the Presbyterian Historical Society offers digital access to a number of periodicals through a separate Magazine Membership. The publications in question are:

The Orthodox Presbyterian, 1829–40
The Covenanter, 1830–43
The Bible Christian, 1830–45
The Presbyterian Penny Magazine, 1834–37
Young Men's Magazine, 1858–59

9.3 Missionary magazines

Early magazines with a focus on missionary work include the *Monthly Missionary Herald*, which began in 1837. In 1842 this magazine was taken over by the Mission Board of the General Assembly and renamed the *Missionary Herald*. The British Newspaper Archive (www.britishnewspaperarchive.co.uk) currently provides online access to the 12 issues of this magazine issued in 1855. The *Missionary Herald* continued until 1942 when it merged with *The Irish Presbyterian*, which had first appeared in 1895. The new magazine was called *The Presbyterian Herald*, which continues to be published to this day. The BNA has also digitised the *Monitor, and Missionary Chronicle, of the Reformed Presbyterian Church in Ireland* for the years 1853–5. In addition to the obvious focus on the work of missionaries, these periodicals can include information on those supporting missionary endeavours. For example, the issue of 1 March 1855 of the *Monitor, and Missionary Chronicle* includes the names of the contributors to the Knockbracken Juvenile Missionary Association – valuable information for a congregation for which there are few other records of this era. See also Professor Barkley's article, 'The Overseas Missionary Magazines of the Irish Presbyterian Church' in the 1977 edition of the *BPHSI*.

9.4 *The Banner of Ulster*

While some newspapers drew a majority of their readership from the broader Presbyterian community and were considered to be supportive of or sympathetic towards the causes favoured by Presbyterians – examples include the *Northern Whig*, founded in 1824, and the *Londonderry Standard*, established in 1836 – arguably the first newspaper to be produced specifically for Presbyterians in Ireland was the *Banner of Ulster*. Coinciding with the two-hundredth anniversary of the formation of the first Irish Presbytery, the *Banner of Ulster* appeared for the first time on 10 June 1842 as a twice-weekly publication. Its first editorial declared that its intention was to 'advance the interests of the Presbyterian Church'. The newspaper carried a broad range of news items with an obvious focus on the activities of the Presbyterian churches. As was the case with other newspapers, notices of births, deaths and marriages were included as well as obituaries. An example of the latter was published in the *Banner of Ulster* on 6 December 1844:

On the 29th ultimo, in the sixty-third year of her age Eleanor Bevan Spear, eldest daughter of the late William Spear, Esq., Spearvale, Co. Cavan, deeply and deservedly lamented by her relatives and a numerous circle of acquaintances, to whom she had endeared herself by her urbanity of manners and kindness of disposition. This excellent person was warm, yet sincere, in her friendship – charitable, yet unostentatious in her benevolence. To her the tale of woe was never related in vain – from her door the object of charity was never dismissed unrelieved. In this she followed the footsteps of her late inestimable mother, since whose death, in 1825, she discharged her duties in the Spearvale domestic circle in such manner as to command the respect and ensure the love of every member of the family. She bore long and severe illness with great fortitude and Christian patience. She earnestly longed to be 'absent from the body, and present with the Lord;' and amidst the sufferings of her body, the aspirations of her soul were, 'Lord Jesus, receive my spirit.'

The *Banner of Ulster* continued until 31 August 1869. Its full surviving run – 3,669 issues – is available online through the British Newspaper Archive.

9.5 *The Witness*

Though there was a five-year interval between the one ceasing and the other commencing, *The Witness* has often been called the successor to the *Banner of Ulster*. Published weekly, *The Witness* began in 1874 under the editorship of Alexander McMonagle, a native of Londonderry, who had previously worked on a number of newspapers, including the *Banner of Ulster*. McMonagle continued in post until his death in 1919. For most of this time he combined his editorship of *The Witness* with that of the *Ulster Echo*, a daily evening newspaper aimed at Presbyterians, until the latter ceased in 1916. McMonagle was succeeded as editor of *The Witness* by John F. Charlesson. Owing to the wartime conditions, *The Witness* was published for the last time in January 1941. Although there were some hopes that it would be revived after the war, this was not to be. Professor Barkley expressed the views of many when he wrote that the demise of *The Witness* was 'a tragedy not only for the Church but for the community ... never to mention the historian' (*BPHSI* (1974), p. 9).

The Witness included a broad range of news items with an obvious emphasis on items that would appeal to Presbyterians. Extensive coverage was given to Presbyterian meetings and events, from the sittings of the General Assembly to Sunday school outings, and many personal announcements of births, deaths and marriages were included. Copies of *The Witness* can be found in different archives and libraries, including the British Library and Linen Hall Library. The most comprehensive set of issues is available in the Presbyterian Historical Society, where it can be viewed on microfilm. The PHSI has been extracting birth, marriage and death notices from *The Witness* and adding these to its website for members of the Society.

9.6 Overseas Presbyterian publications

Researchers should also consider the possibility of finding information on an ancestor in a periodical published by a Presbyterian denomination in another part of the world. Such magazines have been exploited successfully by many people in search of their roots. To take the Reformed Presbyterian Church as an example, an outstanding online resource has been created by the History Committee of the Reformed Presbyterian Church of North America (http://rparchives.org). This includes digital scans of many Reformed Presbyterian periodicals published in the United States, including the *Reformed Presbyterian* (1837–62), *Covenanter* (1845–62) and *Reformed Presbyterian and Covenanter* (1863–95), among others. These periodicals include obituaries, many of which concern individuals born in Ireland. By way of example, the following obituary appeared in the *Reformed Presbyterian and Covenanter* in 1869 (vol. 7, p. 285):

The subject of this notice James Witherspoon died in the city of New York April 14th 1869. The deceased was born in county Down Ireland June 20th 1789. His parents were members of Knockbracken congregation and he was baptized by Rev. William Stavely one of the well known fathers of the church. The family emigrated to this country in the year 1804, the deceased as well as most of the family remaining residents of the city of New York. He was through life warmly attached to the principles of the Reformed Presbyterian Church and was at the time of his death a member of the Third congregation in that city. For a number of years he was a victim of disease suffering specially from asthma and general debility. After these years of affliction he literally fell asleep in Jesus without pain or struggle. His latter end was eminently peace. He leaves an aged and feeble widow who mourns her loss and feels very deeply her desolateness. Two daughters also survive him He was a lover of the truth a lover of good men bearing meekly his trials sustained by that grace of God that bringeth salvation.

What the obituary does not say is that Witherspoon's father James was banished from Ireland as a result of his involvement in planning the failed rebellion of Robert Emmet in 1803, having a few years before this fought for the insurgents in the 1798 Rebellion. Another useful resource on the rparchives.org website is a set of abstracts of obituaries in the *Covenanter* for the years 1845–62, compiled by James H. Sterrett in 1977. A significant proportion of these are of people born in Ireland. For example, Thomas McClurkin senior, who died in Illinois in 1845, had been born near Ballymoney, County Antrim, and had emigrated to South Carolina where he fought in the Revolutionary war. The website also includes printed minutes of Synod from its commencement in 1809 and information on the history of the denomination and details on its ministers.

10

Presbyterians and education

The house was a thatched cabin. The seats were black oak sticks from the neighbouring bog. A fire of peat blazed, or rather smoked, in the middle of the floor, and a hole in the roof served for a chimney. The teacher was a Mr Joseph Pollock, or Poak, as he was familiarly called – a tall Scotchman ... a Presbyterian, of the "straitest sect" ...

The first school attended by Rev. Henry Cooke (b. 1788)[1]

10.1 The emphasis on education

Presbyterians have always placed a high premium on education, not only in terms of an educated ministry, but also in having a literate membership. This chapter does not attempt to provide a comprehensive survey of the subject, but outlines briefly the role of Presbyterians in education and the records that are available. Many Presbyterian clergymen organised their own schools, sometimes while waiting to take up a ministerial position. One of the earliest of these was the school established by Rev. James McAlpine at Killyleagh in 1697 where Rev. Francis Hutcheson, later Professor of Moral Philosophy at Glasgow University, received some of his early education. In the second half of the eighteenth century notable academies were founded at Rademon by Rev. Moses Neilson and at Strabane by Rev. William Crawford. Unfortunately very few records of these institutions have survived.

The driving force behind the establishment of Belfast Academy (now Belfast Royal Academy) in 1786 was Rev. Dr James Crombie. A Scotsman, Crombie was the minister of the First Presbyterian congregation and his ambition was to establish a school along the lines of a Scottish collegiate institution. Copies of the first minute books of the academy, covering the years 1786–1880 are in PRONI (T3101).[2] Presbyterian ministers continued to organise and teach in schools of their own in the nineteenth century. PRONI holds account books of the school conducted by Rev. Charles James McAlester of First Holywood (Non-Subscribing), 1842–57 and 1874–85 (D3686). These include the names of the pupils attending the school as well as the fees they paid for tuition and teaching materials, etc. The widow of a Presbyterian minister, Margaret Byers, was a pioneer of female education in Ireland, founding a school for girls in Belfast in 1859. A purpose-built facility for her Ladies Collegiate School was built in 1873–4 and in 1887 the school was renamed Victoria College. In recognition of her achievements Byers was awarded an honorary doctorate by the University of Dublin in 1905.[3]

10.2 Sunday schools

Around 1770, at Doagh in County Antrim, a Presbyterian named William Galt founded what is considered to be the first Sunday school in Ireland. Others would follow, including one in Belfast taught by one of the leaders of the United Irishmen, Henry Joy McCracken. These schools provided more than religious instruction, with lessons in literacy and numeracy. In 1809 the Hibernian Sunday School Society was formed. An interdenominational and voluntary association, which enjoyed strong support from Presbyterians, it was renamed the Sunday School Society for Ireland in 1815. In the 1830s the Synod of Ulster and the Secession Synod encouraged the formation of congregational Sunday schools. In 1862 a Presbyterian Sabbath School Society was established, the history of which is told in J. M. Barkley, *The Sabbath School Society for Ireland, 1862–1962* (1961).

For documents relating to Presbyterian Sunday schools, see the PRONI *Guide to Church Records* and the listings of congregational records created by the Presbyterian Historical Society (see Chapter 3.4). To give a few examples, among the records of Second Portglenone, is a Sunday school roll book, 1821–67 (MIC1P/357). The records for First Antrim (Millrow) include a Sabbath school receipt and expenditure book, 1835–62, incorporating a weekly roll of teachers and salaries, 1840–41 (CR3/2/B/6). PRONI also holds the minute book of Rathfryland Presbyterian Sunday school, 1833–80

(T1537/1). These records can be illuminating about the nature of the education offered as well as providing details on the children who were taught. The Sunday school register for New Row Presbyterian Church in Coleraine, covering the years 1837–51, provides the names, addresses, ages and reading abilities of the pupils (MIC1P/31/1).

10.3 Day schools

Many Presbyterian congregations established day schools. These met in different settings, including the meeting house, Session-house, private homes and in purpose-built structures. One of the earliest was the boys' school in the First Presbyterian Church in Belfast, which was in existence by 1762. The subjects taught at it included reading, writing and singing – the boys formed a choir in the meeting house – and the pupils were clothed with the costs met by an annual charity sermon. It was noted in 1771 that the schoolmaster, a Mr Crawford, had emigrated to America; in the meantime the boys were taught by his wife.[4] A 'Blue Coat' school was organised by First Derry c. 1773. Here too the boys led the singing in the meeting house.[5] The supervision of these schools was generally the responsibility of the minister and Session and information on them can be found in congregational minute books. Rarely, however, are the names of pupils recorded unless there were specific reasons for them to be mentioned. The Session minutes of First Derry record the following absentees from the 'Blue Coat' school on 5 December 1814: William Grey (scarlet fever and measles), James and William Kennedy, and Alan Bryans (all measles).[6]

In the early nineteenth century there was a growing demand for education and the number of schools increased significantly. However, the quality of the instruction was variable and the school buildings (as the above description of Rev. Henry Cooke's first school indicates) were often poor.[7] A major step forward in the provision of schooling in Ireland was the formation by the government of the Board of Commissioners for National Education in 1831. The Board provided state support for local initiatives to provide schooling, contributing money to assist with the building of schools and the salaries of teachers, as well as operating an inspectorate and publishing text books. Schools supported and regulated in this way were known as National Schools. To begin with there was strong opposition to the

National system from many within the Synod of Ulster who were concerned at the failure to recognise the centrality of the Bible to teaching. However, by 1840 the government had accepted the main demands of the Synod, allowing Presbyterians to run their own schools in line with their religious scruples, but avail, if they wished to do so, of the support on offer from the National Board.

Presbyterians were not uniformly hostile to the National system in its early years and some tried to work with the National Board. For example, Rev. James Porter, the minister of the Secession congregation of Drumlee, was a supporter of the National system, though this provoked much opposition. According to his grandson, speaking in 1939, 'When he put Drumlee [school] under the National Board the opposition was so great that police had to be brought to protect the teacher and even Mr Porter from violence.'[8] It was not until 1861 that there was a further application to the National Board on behalf of Drumlee school. In this application there was an acknowledgement that the local people had been 'heretofore much opposed to the principles of the Board, but now anxious to partake of the advantages which it offers' (ED/1/17/101).

The Public Record Office of Northern Ireland and the National Archives of Ireland hold extensive collections of records relating to the National system of education, including grant aid applications, correspondence registers and salary books (in both institutions these records are catalogued under the prefix ED). Through these it is possible to explore the Presbyterian contribution to schools supported by the National Board. Taking the example of grant aid applications, the forms for completion included a series of questions about the school, covering such matters as the date it was founded, the condition of the building in which classes were conducted, the name of the teacher and the number of pupils in attendance. The applications in PRONI can be downloaded via the archive's online eCatalogue. By way of example, a grant aid application from the Killead Meeting House School, dating from 1833 (an example of early Presbyterian support for the National system) is in PRONI (ED/1/1/72).

The application reveals that the school, which was in the townland of Tully, had been established more than 30 years earlier. The building was constructed of stone with a slated roof and measured 24 feet by 18 feet. The school was solely under the superintendence of the

Presbyterian minister and his Session and the pupils, with one exception, were Presbyterians. In summer 23 boys and seven girls attended, while in winter the figures were 25 boys and 15 girls. Five days each week were 'devoted to combined moral & literary education'. Saturday and an hour on each of the other days were set aside for reading the Bible and learning the Catechism. The school building seems to have doubled as the Session-house for it was noted that it was used by the minister and elders on Sundays. The teacher, John McKain, received his income from the fees paid by the pupils (five shillings per quarter). The aid sought from the National Board was for improving the teacher's salary, thereby allowing children to attend the school who could not afford the current fees. The signatories supporting the application were the minister of Killead, Rev. Joseph McKee, three members of the Session and four members of the congregational committee.

PRONI holds the records of more than 1,500 National (later Public Elementary) schools, which have been catalogued under SCH. In the Republic of Ireland the National Archives has some school records, with others in county archives, libraries and museums. Most pupil enrolment registers survive from no earlier than the late 1860s. These record the name, age and residence of the child, the date of entrance, and the occupation of the child's father or guardian (unfortunately not the name of the parents).

As noted above, information on schools can be found in congregational records, though seldom will the names of children appear. A rare example of an early nineteenth-century school register is that of Magherally school, covering the years 1824–8 (MIC1P/211/1). The register includes details of the classes, as well as the date the child left the school. On occasion the reason for the departure is given, such as death or emigration to America. One large blank space is headed 'use this for sketching out sermons'.[9] The records of Ulsterville Presbyterian Church, Belfast, in the Presbyterian Historical Society include an account book of Ulsterville National School, 1914–23. Among the records of First Carrickfergus is the minute book of the Building Committee of Lancasterian Street School, 1879–81 (MIC1P/157/3). Congregational histories can be a useful source of information on schools run under the auspices of the Presbyterian Church.

10.4 Congregational libraries

A further expression of the aim of Presbyterians to provide greater access to learning was the creation of libraries by many congregations. The records of Second Ballynahinch include a library subscription list for 1836–7 (MIC1P/110/4), while for First Antrim there is a Sabbath School library loan book, 1870 and 1879–81 (MIC1P/3/3). The records of Dundalk Presbyterian Church in the National Library of Ireland include a register of books borrowed from the congregational library, 1879–81 and 1886–94 (MS 33,682). A library loan account book covering the years 1886–9 is available for Ballee Non-Subscribing Presbyterian Church (MIC1B/3/1).

10.5 University education

Prior to the early nineteenth century, most Irish Presbyterians who availed of a third level education did so in Scotland, with few attending the Anglican-dominated Trinity College Dublin. A majority seem to have been educated at the University of Glasgow – where they are sometimes listed as 'Scoto-Hibernus' – and records of students at this institution can be found in the following publications: *Munimenta Alme Universitatis Glasguensis: Records of the University of Glasgow from its Foundation Till 1727*, edited by Joseph Robertson and Cosmo Innes (4 vols, 1854); *The Matriculation Albums of the University of Glasgow from 1728 to 1858*, transcribed and annotated by W. Innes Addison (1913). For students at the University of Edinburgh, see *A Catalogue of the Graduates in the Faculties of Arts, Divinity, and Law, of the University of Edinburgh, Since its Foundation 1583* (1858).

Students were issued with certificates testifying that they had completed a session of lectures at the university. Three certificates issued to John Thomson, a student at the University of Glasgow, are reproduced in Robert Bonar's history of Carnmoney Presbyterian Church.[10] One, dated 27 April 1764, states that Thomson had 'attended the lectures both on Moral Philosophy and on the Greek language one hour each day'. The certificate, which was written by James Moor, Professor of Greek, goes on to note that 'his attendance and the whole of his behaviour has been to the satisfaction of the teachers of both these classes'.

10.6 Belfast Inst

The founding of 'Inst' – Belfast Academical Institution (the prefix Royal was added in 1831) – with its Collegiate Department provided an opportunity for Presbyterians to receive a higher education without having to leave Ireland. The Collegiate Department, which opened in 1815, included professorships in such subjects as Mathematics, Moral Philosophy, and Greek, Latin and Hebrew. Those who completed their studies successfully were awarded a General Certificate, which was accepted by the Synod of Ulster and Secession Synods as the equivalent of a degree conferred by a university. Furthermore, the management of Inst invited the Presbyterian bodies to appoint their own professors of theology to the Collegiate Department. The first appointee of the Synod of Ulster was Rev. Samuel Hanna, while the Seceders chose Rev. Samuel Edgar. With the opening of Queen's College Belfast in 1849, the Collegiate Department at Inst closed. For more on the story of Inst, see John Jamieson, *The History of the Royal Belfast Academical Institution, 1810–1960* (1960).

PRONI holds an extensive collection of records for Belfast Inst, both for the School Department and the Collegiate Department (SCH/524). Information on attendees is contained in a series of 'Albums'. Those for the Collegiate Department cover the years 1815–37 (SCH/524/1A/6) and 1838–48 (SCH/524/1A/7). The information provided includes name of student; name and occupation of father; place of residence; presbytery with which associated; subjects studied and the years in which they were taken; and details of subsequent career (not all of these details are provided in every case). The Collegiate Department catered for a much broader range of students than those who were intending to go into the Presbyterian ministry. Nonetheless, the impact that it had on the Church can be gauged from the *Fasti* and the number of ministers who are listed as having attended 'O.C.B.' (Old College Belfast, as the Collegiate Department came to be referred to).

By way of example, George Jardine, who attended the Collegiate Department during the years 1817–23, was the son of John Jardine, a farmer near Banbridge. Prior to attending Inst, George had been taught by Rev. Mr Lunn of Greenhill; Lunn was probably James Lunn from Magherally, who had been licensed to preach in 1803, though was not ordained minister of a congregation until 1821 when he became pastor of Carlingford. The Inst records note that George Jardine was licensed by the Dromore Presbytery and emigrated to America. Taking another example, Thomas Smith, son of Samuel Smith, a Belfast merchant, was a student from 1825 to 1829. He then taught at Inst briefly before going to the Independent Seminary at Homerton, near London, and then emigrating to America in 1830 where he went on to serve as a Presbyterian minister in Charleston, South Carolina.

10.7 The Presbyterian College

Concerns emanating from the conservative wing of the Synod of Ulster, shared by the Seceders, over the appointment of liberal Presbyterians to professorships in the Collegiate Department of Belfast Inst came to the fore in the 1820s and worsened in the 1830s. Eventually, in 1841, the General Assembly resolved to 'seek a college for the education of her ministers over which she shall have adequate authority and control'.[11] However, more than a decade passed before this became a physical reality. Eventually opened in 1853, the Presbyterian College – also known as Assembly's College – was erected on a site close to Queen's College Belfast. The first president was the redoubtable Rev. Dr Henry Cooke, who was also one of the original professors.

In 1881 the Presbyterian Theological Faculty of Ireland – comprising the theological professors of the Presbyterian College and of Magee College (see next) – was incorporated by royal charter with the power to confer degrees in theology. The present name of the college – Union Theological College – was acquired in 1978 after the merger with Magee. For the history of the seminary in its first hundred years, see Robert Allen, *The Presbyterian College Belfast, 1853–1953* (1953). Allen's book contains a list of the students at the college from its opening. It is arranged by year of entry and gives the name of the student and his or her qualifications. A transcription of this list is available on the PHSI website (members only). The College includes the Gamble Library, opened in 1873, with its magnificent collections of publications and manuscripts to which reference is made elsewhere in this book.

10.8 Magee College

Magee College was established in the city of Derry using the generous bequest of £20,000 by Martha Magee, the widow of Rev. William

Magee of Lurgan. It opened in 1865 and offered courses in both arts and theology. Though established as a Presbyterian institution with a strong emphasis on preparing men for the ministry, it accepted students from all backgrounds and from 1878 admitted women. In 1907, following a large bequest from Basil McCrea, the institution was renamed McCrea Magee College and in 1909 a relationship was established with Trinity College Dublin. Further developments in the twentieth century included the creation of Magee University College following the separation of the arts and theology departments in the 1950s. The former became part of what is now Ulster University and the latter merged with the Presbyterian College, Belfast, in 1978 to create Union Theological College.

Records of the Magee University College Presbyterian Trust are held by PRONI (MPT). These include minute books of faculty and of the trustees which cover such subjects as the admission of students, staff appointments, discipline, examinations and prizes. Other records include account books. Studies of the college include John R. Leebody, *A Short History of M'Crea Magee College, Derry, During its First Fifty Years* (1915) and R. F. G. Holmes, *Magee 1865–1965: The Evolution of the Magee Colleges* (1965). Leebody's book includes a chronological list of students at Magee (available for members on the PHSI website).

Notes

[1] J. L. Porter, *Life and Times of Henry Cooke* (1875), pp 3–4; the school was at Ballymacilcurr, near Maghera, County Londonderry.

[2] The early history of the school is very well dealt with in A. T. Q. Stewart, *Belfast Royal Academy: The First Century, 1785–1885* (1985), which includes the names of the original patrons/subscribers in 1785 (pp 102–03). Other histories include Hugh Shearman, *Belfast Royal Academy 1785–1935* (1935) and Edward McCamley, *Belfast Royal Academy: The Second Century 1885–1985* (1996).

[3] See Alison Jordan's biography, *Margaret Byers*, published by the Institute of Irish Studies at QUB, which draws extensively on the school's own archives.

[4] Gordon, *First Presbyterian Church in Belfast*, p. 116.

[5] Young, *First Derry*, pp 21–2. The term 'Blue Coat' derives from the colour of the coats worn by the boys.

6 Ibid., p. 22.

7 In 1824 Rev. Robert Park, minister of First Ballymoney, prepared a detailed report of the schools in the parish of Ballymoney for the commission enquiring into education in Ireland, a copy of which is in PRONI (D499/1). The document has been published: David Kennedy, 'Select documents V. Robert Park's Account of Schools in Ballymoney Parish, 1824', *Irish Historical Studies*, vol. 6, no. 21 (March 1948), pp 23–43.

8 Quoted in Truesdale, *Drumlee*, pp 43–4.

9 Martin, *Magherally*, p. 45.

10 Bonar, *Carnmoney*, p. 36.

11 Holmes, *Our Irish Presbyterian Heritage*, p. 127.

11

Other sources of information on Presbyterians

This chapter provides a summary overview of a selection of additional records that may be useful in researching Presbyterian ancestors. Some of these concern Presbyterians *as Presbyterians*, though others are more general. For a more in-depth look at the sources highlighted below as well as many others, see John Grenham, *Tracing Your Irish Ancestors* (5th edition, 2019) and William Roulston, *Researching Scots-Irish Ancestors: The Essential Genealogical Guide to Early Modern Ulster, 1600–1800* (2nd edition, 2018).

11.1 Landed estate papers

For much of the last four centuries the majority of Presbyterians have earned their living from the land. While the proportion of Presbyterians engaged in farming is not as high as it once was, nonetheless the backbone of many rural congregations is still composed of farming families. Until the beginning of the twentieth century the most important unit of land organisation in Ireland was the estate. Very few farmers owned their farms outright, but rather leased them from a landlord. The various plantation schemes, followed by the Cromwellian, Restoration and Williamite land settlements of the 1650s through to the beginning of the eighteenth century all contributed to the evolution of the landed estate system. It was not until the passing of a series of acts of parliament in the late nineteenth and early twentieth centuries that these estates were broken up and an owner-occupier class of farmers was created.

The documents generated by the management of landed estates – especially rentals, leases, lease books, maps, correspondence and manor court records – are among the most valuable records for the family historian. There are two main repositories for documentation relating to estates in Ireland: the Public Record Office of Northern

Ireland and the National Library of Ireland. Estate papers can also be found in the National Archives of Ireland and the Manuscripts & Archives Research Library of Trinity College Dublin. County archives and libraries in the Republic of Ireland also hold collections of estate papers. Some examples are given below to highlight the importance of estate collections for research into Presbyterian farming ancestors.

The extensive eighteenth-century correspondence generated by the Abercorn estate in counties Donegal and Tyrone includes a number of letters concerning Presbyterian congregations. By way of example, on 26 January 1778 a land surveyor named John Hood wrote to the Earl of Abercorn on behalf of the Presbyterian congregation of Monreagh in County Donegal (D623/A/43/85). The meeting house of this congregation stood on land that had been provided by the Abercorns. Hood's letter revealed that a dispute had arisen between the congregation and a Hugh Rankin over the ground adjoining the meeting house:

> The fact is Hugh Rankin gave it out that though we had got the Green, he had got the grass, from your Lordship. He was interrogated in the session, if he was serious, which he AVOWED. His assertions however gained little credit until yesterday, that a gap was perceived, laid open between the green and one of his fields, which we understood as a formal entry upon the premises. This aroused us, and the congregation stayed after public worship, to "canvas" the affair a little better, when on his being further interrogated he declined affirming, the call was too sudden and the place to[o] solemn perhaps to l[ie]! But he could not be prevailed on to drop his pretensions. The congregation therefore resolved to acquaint your Lordship with his conduct. It is, to be sure, of no great value, a cow's grass! But it is an article which we cannot want.

Hood further related some details concerning a previous minister, Rev. William Boyd, who had died in 1772:

> Our connections with the late Rev. Mr Boyd's dwelling, where our sexton, and our horses were formerly accommodated, are by his death, and its division amongst his sons-in-law broke off. And we have built a stable, and a house for the sexton on the Green, in a taste becomming the estate and the congregation to which it belongs. He cannot live comfortably without a milch cow, and it is well able to

graze one. We held it without reserve, and we make no doubt the noble donor intended not. We hope and believe these considerations will outweigh whatever may be suggested against us. I am, my Lord, with the most profound respect and veneration and in behalf of my deputants, your Lordship's obedient obliged humble servant.

Finally, Hood, believing that it would give the landlord 'more refined delight than greater things from another quarter', informed Lord Abercorn that: 'We intend to perpetuate the memory of your munificient gifts to us, and our gratitude to you by erecting a clock in our meetinghouse inscribed to your Lordship.'

Among other records of interest, the Downshire Papers in PRONI include a petition from Captain Arthur MacMahon on board *The Veteran* prison ship near Gosport, England, to the Dowager Marchioness of Downshire, dated 20 February 1810 (D671/C/12/55). In great detail MacMahon described how he had been victimised by the Stewart family during the election in County Down in 1790 over claims that he had influenced his son to vote against Robert Stewart (later Lord Castlereagh). At this time MacMahon had been the Presbyterian minister of Kilrea, County Londonderry. He went on to relate his subsequent experiences, including the accusations that he was a United Irishman. The Farnham papers in the National Library of Ireland include correspondence relating to the construction of a Presbyterian meeting house in the town of Cavan, 1835 (MS 41,146/45).

Irish estate collections can also be found in archives in Great Britain.[1] During research in what was then the Nottingham County Record Office (now the Nottinghamshire Archives) in the summer of 1978 Jack Johnston discovered a petition from 'a considerable number of the Protestant Descenting [sic] tenants of the Manor of Cecil' to their landlord, F. F. Foljambe. Though undated, it would appear to have been drawn up around 1807. The petition concerned the allocation of a small amount of land surrounding the meeting house to the congregation. The petitioners lamented that they were weak financially and their place of worship was 'in very bad repair' and hoped that Foljambe would be able to provide assistance to them. Nineteen men signed the petition, a transcription of which is included in Jack Johnston's history of Glenhoy, along with a facsimile reproduction of the original document.[2]

The collection of records of the Meade estate in County Down in the Norfolk Record Office contains several items relating to local congregations. These include:

> Signed memorial addressed to Lt General the Hon. R. Meade from the Presbyterians at Rathfriland, requesting a site for a new meeting house and burial ground, 1833 (MEA5/40)
>
> Petition of Minister and Committee of First Presbyterian Congregation at Rathfriland for funds towards debt incurred by extensive alterations, 1835 (MEA5/41)
>
> Memorial from tenants in Derrydummuck, Ballinagross and Shankhill and members of the Presbyterian Congregation of Glascar concerning funds to erect a school house, 1848 (MEA5/50)
>
> Memorial from Presbyterian Congregation of Loughbrickland concerning funds to furnish the meetinghouse and erect a schoolhouse, 1852 (MEA5/58)

11.2 Petitions of Protestant Dissenters, 1775

In 1774, an act was passed in the Irish Parliament which restricted the voting rights of non-conformists at vestry meetings. This provoked a huge outcry from Presbyterians and nearly 40 petitions protesting against this legislation were submitted to the government in October and November 1775. Most of these petitions emanated from Presbyterian congregations, though some members of the Established Church also voiced their opposition. In 1776 the act was repealed through a bill introduced by Thomas Conolly, whose own tenants in County Londonderry had been particularly vociferous in their opposition to the original act.

The original petitions were destroyed, but transcripts made by Tenison Groves are available in PRONI (T808/15307). Only the names of the petitioners are given, not where they lived. The names in these transcripts can now be searched online via the PRONI Name Search database. The congregations and parishes for which there are petitions with names are set out below.

> County Antrim – Antrim Borough; Old Antrim [possibly the non-subscribing congregation]; Ballyclare town and neighbourhood; Ballymena town and neighbourhood; Belfast parish and town; Carnmoney parish; Carrickfergus town and county; Donagore,

Kilbride and Nilteen; Dunmurry congregation in Drumbeg parish; Larne, Raloo, Carncastle, Kilwaughter, Glenarm & Ballyeaston; Lisburn town and neighbourhood

County Armagh – Armagh parish; Clare congregation in Ballymore parish

County Down – Ballee congregation; Comber parish; Dundonald parish; Dromore parish; Drumara parish; Drumballyroney and Drumgoolan parishes; Drumgooland; Killileagh parish

County Londonderry – Coleraine and Killowen parishes; Londonderry City

County Tyrone – Benburb town and neighbourhood; Coagh; Cookstown congregation; Dungannon barony; Dungannon town and neighbourhood; Strabane town and neighbourhood

11.3 Official records in the National Archives of Ireland

Established in 1988 through the amalgamation of the Public Record Office of Ireland and the State Paper Office in Dublin Castle, the National Archives of Ireland (NAI) is the official repository of governmental records relating to the Republic of Ireland. The records deriving from the former State Paper Office include the **Rebellion Papers**, which together comprise the most important source of information on the United Irishmen and the 1798 Rebellion. While the records in this collection predominantly relate to the period 1796–1805, there are some from either side of those years. The Rebellion Papers include a broad range of documentation, ranging from letters and petitions to lists of prisoners and records of court martials. Since many Presbyterians, including ministers, were involved, or at least implicated, in the United Irishmen and the events of 1798 the Rebellion Papers have the potential to include information on Presbyterian ancestors. By way of example, a list of prisoners held in Belfast in September 1798 is mainly composed of Presbyterians, including two ministers – Rev. William Steel Dickson of Portaferry and Rev. William Stavely, a Covenanter minister based at Knockbracken near Belfast (RP 620/4/29/36).

The voluminous **Chief Secretary's Office Registered Papers** (CSORP) cover the period 1818–1924 and include letters, petitions and reports submitted to the Chief Secretary, the most senior official in the Irish administration after the Lord Lieutenant. A project to catalogue these papers for the years 1818–52 is ongoing. A few examples follow of records relating to Presbyterians. Dating from 1819 is a letter from Rev. Samuel Butler, Presbyterian minister of Magilligan, County Londonderry, concerning the possibility of government assistance for voluntary emigration to New South Wales since, if this was available, many of the poor in his area would be interested (CSO/RP/1819/74). In 1828 the Secession congregation of Carnone in County Donegal submitted a petition to the Chief Secretary concerning the *Regium Donum* (CSO/RP/1824/2109). The petition, which was signed by 15 people, stated that Carnone was the second largest congregation in the county with 137 families. From 1828–9 is a collection of documents concerning the character and conduct of a policeman in the Garvagh-Kilrea area of County Londonderry, including two lengthy lists of petitioners (CSO/RP/1829/325). Rev. James Brown, Presbyterian minister of First Garvagh played a prominent role in this episode, which is looked at in more detail in an article by Linde Lunney in *Directory of Irish Family History Research*, no. 42 (2019).

The records of Chief Secretary's Office also include the collection known as the **Official Papers** (OP), comprising correspondence and other documentation. Series 1 covers material from 1790 to 1831, and Series 2 from 1832 to 1880. Within Series 1 is a petition (undated, but almost certainly from 1828) from the Presbyterian congregation of Balteagh, County Londonderry, concerning the *Regium Donum*. This lists the names of the head of each household and the children in that household (though only rarely is the name of the wife given). This petition is all the more valuable since the surviving register of baptisms of this congregation begins in 1868. The petition was the subject of an article by Steven Smyrl in the *Irish Genealogist* in 2011.

An additional set of documentation within the records of the Chief Secretary's Office has been termed **Official Papers, Miscellaneous Assorted** (1780–1882). This includes a number of items relating to Presbyterians. For example, the collection includes two issues of the printed journal of Rev. James Carlile to the members of the Scots' Church in Capel Street, Dublin, dated 25 March 1842 and 21 May 1842 (CSO/OPMA/1370). These give some personal details of the issues facing his congregation. One further item to mention is a file from the records of the Department of Foreign Affairs titled 'The Protestant and the Presbyterian contribution to the Irish revolutionary movement', 1953 (DFA/5/305/14/258).

11.4 Newspapers

It has long been recognised that newspapers have the potential to be excellent sources of information on family history. In recent years digitisation is providing ever greater access to old newspapers, dramatically improving the ease with which they can be used. Two major online providers are the British Newspaper Archive (www.britishnewspaperarchive.co.uk) and the Irish Newspaper Archives (www.irishnewsarchive.com). A comprehensive record of the availability of Irish newspapers in archives and libraries in the British Isles is contained in the NEWSPLAN database, which can be accessed via the website of the National Library of Ireland (www.nli.ie/en/catalogues-and-databases-printed-newspapers.aspx). By far, the most important newspaper published in Ulster in the eighteenth century was the *Belfast Newsletter* which first appeared in September 1737. A comprehensive index to the surviving issues of the *Belfast Newsletter* from 1738 to 1800 (there are many gaps in its early years) is available on the Internet: www.ucs.louisiana.edu/bnl.

As noted elsewhere, Presbyterian gatherings, especially ordinations and the meetings of the higher courts of the church received coverage in the press, especially from the early 1800s onwards. On occasion, newspapers can include invaluable listings of names of members of a congregation, drawn up in response to particular occurrences. A few eighteenth-century examples are given below:

> Resolution of members of Markethill Presbyterian Church deploring current disorder – *Belfast Newsletter*, 9 Aug. 1763
> Memorial opposing the Hearts of Steel by the congregation of Moneyrea – *Belfast Newsletter*, 3 April 1772
> Subscribers to a reward fund by members of Cullybackey Presbyterian Church – *Belfast Newsletter*, 8 Jan. 1773
> Subscribers to a reward fund by members of the 'Protestant Dissenting Congregation of Donaghmore' (County Down) – *Belfast Newsletter*, 6–9 Feb. 1776

Apart from Cullybackey none of the other congregations have surviving registers of baptisms and marriages prior to 1800, making these lists of names all the more valuable.

11.5 Civil registration of births, deaths and marriages

As discussed in Chapter 4, civil registration of non-Catholic marriages began on 1 April 1845. This of course included marriages celebrated under the auspices of the Presbyterian churches. The registration of births and deaths as well as Catholic marriages in Ireland began on 1 January 1864. Irish birth certificates do not indicate the religious affiliation of the parents of the child and neither do death certificates state the religion of the deceased. The General Register Office of Ireland (GROI) has copies of births, deaths and marriages for all of Ireland from 1845 to 1921 and for the Republic of Ireland from 1922 and records up to a certain date are available online for free (www.irishgenealogy.ie). The General Register Office of Northern Ireland (GRONI) holds the original birth, marriage and death registers recorded by the local district registrars for Northern Ireland. Like GROI, GRONI has made historic records available online, though on a pay-per-view basis (https://geni.nidirect.gov.uk). The Irish Family History Foundation (IFHF) holds at least some civil birth, marriage and death records for the majority of counties in Ireland and these can be accessed by subscribing to the IFHF website (www.rootsireland.ie).

11.6 Census returns

The first census was held in Ireland in 1821 and thereafter every ten years until 1911. Unfortunately, the earliest census that survives in its entirety for the whole of Ireland is the 1901 census. Census returns 1821–51 were almost entirely lost in 1922 in the destruction of the Public Record Office in Dublin. Census returns 1861–91 were completely destroyed by government order, many during the First World War. The original returns of the 1901 and 1911 censuses are deposited at the National Archives in Dublin and are now available online (www.census.nationalarchives.ie), along with surviving fragments from the nineteenth-century census returns. The information in the 1901 census is listed under the following headings: name; relationship to the head of the household; religion; literacy; occupation; age; marital status; county of birth (or country if born outside Ireland); and ability to speak English or Irish. The 1911 census additionally includes the number of years a wife was married, the number of children born and the number still living. It need hardly be said that under the religion heading the word Presbyterian is spelled in umpteen different ways.

11.7 Testamentary records

Prior to 1858 the Church of Ireland was responsible for administering all testamentary affairs. Ecclesiastical or Consistorial Courts in each diocese were responsible for granting probate and conferring on the executors the power to administer the estate. When the estate included property worth more than £5 in another diocese responsibility for the will passed to the Prerogative Court under the authority of the Archbishop of Armagh. It must not be thought that just because the Church of Ireland was responsible for administering wills, only persons who belonged to that particular denomination left wills. Many Presbyterians left wills and if they did not it was principally for economic rather than religious reasons. Unfortunately, nearly all original wills probated before 1858 were destroyed in Dublin in 1922. However, indexes to these destroyed wills do exist and are searchable on the website of the National Archives of Ireland. In addition, the principal repositories in Ireland all have substantial collections of duplicate wills and will abstracts.

The testamentary authority of the Church of Ireland was abolished by the Probate Act of 1857. Testamentary matters were brought under civil jurisdiction and exercised through District Probate Registries and a Principal Registry in Dublin. Bound annual indexes of testamentary papers called 'calendars' were produced and sets of these are available in PRONI and NAI. The district registries retained transcripts of the wills that they proved. Thus, while original wills were destroyed in Dublin in 1922, the transcript copies in will books survived. Both PRONI and NAI have digitised the will books of the district registries (the pre-1904 will transcripts for the Principal Registry were also lost in 1922) in their custody for the period 1858–c. 1900 and these can be searched through the websites of these institutions. Original wills from 1900 onwards are in PRONI or NAI (1904 for Principal Registry wills).

11.8 Electoral records

Prior to 1918 only men could vote and their right to vote depended on various property qualifications. While Catholics were disenfranchised for much of the eighteenth century, Presbyterians were never specifically disbarred from voting in parliamentary elections. Because of their dissent from the political system, Reformed

Presbyterians (Covenanters) would not vote and occasionally this comes across in electoral records. For example, in a 'Deputy Court Cheque Book' for County Antrim of 1776, listing the names of potential voters, the following comment has been added to the entry for John Stevenson of Ballynamaddy: 'wou'd not swear – a Covenanter' (D1364/L/1). The majority of eighteenth- and early nineteenth-century election records have been indexed by PRONI and are available as a searchable database on its website.

In the late nineteenth century there persisted a feeling in certain quarters that Presbyterians were not being treated fairly when it came to civil appointments and public representation. To address these issues the Presbyterian Unionist Voters' Association was created in 1898. It did not last long, but was successful in having one of its candidates, T. L. Corbett, returned to Westminster for the constituency of North Down in 1900. PRONI has a collection of documents relating to the Presbyterian Unionist Voters' Association and its preparations for local government elections in North Antrim in 1898–9 (D2868/D/1). For an exploration of the involvement of Presbyterians in politics in the late nineteenth and early twentieth centuries, see Richard McMinn, 'Presbyterianism and politics in Ulster, 1871–1906', *Studia Hibernica*, vol. 21 (1981), pp 127–46.

11.9 Valuation records

The collection of tithes to support the Church of Ireland clergy was a hugely contentious issue in Ireland. Presbyterians, as well as members of other religious denominations, resented being forced to support the ministers of the Established Church, which was on top of the financial contributions they made to their own pastors. In 1823 the Composition Act was passed which stipulated that henceforth all tithes due to the Church of Ireland, were to be paid in money rather than in kind as they previously could have been. This necessitated a complete valuation of all tithable land in Ireland, the results of which are contained in manuscript form in the tithe applotment books arranged by parish. Original copies of the tithe applotment books are in PRONI and NAI and these have been digitised and made accessible on the websites of these institutions.

The Valuation of Ireland was established by an act of parliament in 1826 and as a result every acre on the island was valued between 1830 and the mid 1860s. Initially, the work was carried out under the aegis of the Townland Valuation before the much more detailed Tenement Valuation was introduced in 1844. The best known of the valuations is the Primary or Griffith's Valuation of 1847–64. For more on these records and the complex process that led to their creation, see Frances McGee, *The Archives of the Valuation of Ireland, 1830–65* (2018). Original valuation records are held in both PRONI and NAI. Many of the manuscript valuation books held by the National Archives of Ireland have been digitised and can be searched on the NAI website. Digital scans of the printed volumes of Griffith's Valuation, along with valuation maps, are available online for free on the Ask About Ireland website (www.askaboutireland.ie/griffith-valuation). PRONI provides online access to digital copies of the Valuation Revision Books of *c.* 1863–*c.* 1930 for Northern Ireland.

11.10 Ordnance Survey Memoirs

Referred to at different points in this book, the Ordnance Survey Memoirs of the 1830s were written accounts intended to accompany the original Ordnance Survey maps. The project was abandoned around 1840 with only the northern part of Ireland covered – principally the province of Ulster and the memoir of only one parish, Templemore in County Londonderry, published. However, in the 1990s the Institute of Irish Studies at Queen's University Belfast published the remaining memoirs in 40 volumes with an additional index volume covering the entire series. The memoirs are most detailed for counties Antrim and Londonderry with 14 volumes each in the Institute of Irish Studies series. By contrast, there is only one volume for County Armagh, while volume 40 of the series covers the material that was produced for counties Cavan, Leitrim, Louth, Monaghan and Sligo.

At their best, the Ordnance Survey Memoirs provide fascinating information on the character and habits of the people of the north of Ireland. The subjects covered include the natural and built environment of antiquities, buildings, fields, hills, lakes and woodlands. There are also sections on the character of the local population, employment and social customs. Religion is also covered, with observations on the proportion of the population of the different religious denominations. Occasional insights into Presbyterians and Presbyterianism can be found, such as the celebration of baptisms and marriages, funeral customs and religious practices. The memoir of the parish of Drummaul, County Antrim, includes the following comments on singing during Presbyterian services:

> At the Presbyterian meeting house the entire congregation join in the singing. The tunes to which their psalms are set are only 12 in number, and are those used by the Covenanters of old. There is something devotional in them, and they are well suited for embracing the variety of voices in a congregation, but at the same time there is a want of harmony or melody in the music at the meeting houses in this parish.[3]

Most parish memoirs include information on public buildings, especially places of worship. The following details concern the Synod of Ulster meeting house in Island Magee, County Antrim:

> The date of the erection of the meeting house cannot be accurately ascertained. 2 very old sundials of stone, one on its western, the other at its southern side, bear the date of 1739, which is supposed to be that of its erection. An old inhabitant named Robert Colville, who died in 1801 at the age of 88 years, stated that when a boy of about 12 years, he assisted in bringing slates in sacks on horseback from the point where they had been landed, for the roofing of the house, and that previous to that time it had been roofed with thatch. The present roof was erected by the congregation in 1838.[4]

11.11 Emigration records

Throughout this book there have been numerous references to emigration and the part played in it by Presbyterians. (See Chapter 7 for a section on Presbyterian ministers and emigration.) Unfortunately, official records of people leaving Ireland do not begin until 1890 and for the 70 years to 1960 these can be searched on the Findmypast website. Prior to 1890, the researcher has to utilise a wide range of records in the search for details of emigration. Chapter 5 has highlighted the ways in which congregational records can provide information on the departure of Presbyterians from Ireland. An invaluable resource is the Irish Emigration Database (IED) created and maintained by the Mellon Centre for Migration Studies (MCMS) at the Ulster American Folk Park, Omagh, County Tyrone. The IED is a computerised collection of over 30,000 records drawn from a variety of mainly eighteenth- and nineteenth-century sources, including emigrant letters, newspaper articles and shipping advertisements. It can be accessed for free via the DIPPAM website (www.dippam.ac.uk). The RootsIreland website (www.rootsireland.ie) hosts the MCMS database of transcriptions of 4,500 ship passenger lists of sailings to North America, 1791–1897 (but mainly 1800–60).

Notes

[1] The Discovery catalogue on the website of The National Archives, London (https://discovery.nationalarchives.gov.uk) covers more than 2,500 archives in the UK and beyond.

[2] Johnston, *Glenhoy*, pp 8–10.

[3] *Ordnance Survey Memoirs of Ireland, Vol. 19: Parishes of County Antrim VI: South-West Antrim* (1993), p. 61.

[4] *Ordnance Survey Memoirs of Ireland, Vol. 10: Parishes of County Antrim III: Larne and Island Magee* (1991), p. 20.

12

Conclusion:
Some research suggestions

Researching Irish Presbyterian ancestors can be as fulfilling or frustrating as investigating forebears from any one of the many other religious denominations on this island. Among the chief frustrations is the fact that relatively few congregations have registers of baptisms and marriages prior to the 1800s. On the other hand, the large number of administrative and other records that were generated by individual congregations and the higher church courts means that it can be possible to put real flesh on the bones of Presbyterian ancestors and so understand more about their social and religious worlds. In the following paragraphs some suggestions are made which researchers may find useful in exploring their family history.

What if I do not know where my Presbyterian ancestors came from?

As researchers are well aware, it is important to know not only the names of one's ancestors, but also the areas in which they lived. The ideal is to know the townland in which the ancestor lived or, if this is not available, the name of the parish. However, for many people the only locational information they have is that their forebear was born somewhere in Ireland, or at best they may know the name of the county. There are obvious difficulties to be overcome here – not necessarily insurmountable, but considerable nonetheless. To have any chance of success it is vital that the place of origin of an ancestor can be narrowed down to a specific area. Answering this question in full is beyond the scope of this book. However, there are some ways of identifying potential places of origin or at least narrowing down where your ancestors might have lived in Ireland.

Two important datasets are discussed in Chapter 11 – the 1901 and 1911 census returns on the website of the National Archives of Ireland (www.census.nationalarchives.ie) and Griffith's Valuation of 1847–64 on the Ask About Ireland website (www.askaboutireland.ie/griffith-valuation). Other indexes to Griffith's Valuation can be found at www.failteromhat.com/griffiths.php and www.rootsireland.ie. These provide an indication of the distribution of surnames across Ireland. Obviously this approach is not particularly helpful for names such as Kelly or Wilson. However, for less common surnames it will be possible to identify places where they are concentrated. For the early 1800s the tithe applotment books can be helpful (discussed under valuation records in Chapter 11).

Prior to the early nineteenth century the task is much more difficult. The most extensive single source from the late 1700s is the list of over 56,000 names (36,000+ for Ulster) of those who applied for flaxseed premiums in 1796. These applicants, as well as names from some other early sources, can be accessed via the Ulster Historical Foundation's website (www.ancestryireland.com/scotsinulster). In addition, the websites of PRONI (go to the Name Search database) and NAI (www.genealogy.nationalarchives.ie) include a number of datasets of sources that date from or include the seventeenth and eighteenth centuries. For more on pre-1800 sources for Ulster, see William J. Roulston, *Researching Scots-Irish Ancestors* (2nd edition, 2018).

Identifying the relevant congregation

Some people are in the fortunate position of knowing the congregation to which their ancestors belonged. They may have a certificate of disjunction issued to their ancestor by his or her congregation on their departure to another part of the world. Or they may have a volume presented to their ancestor which contains a book-plate stating the name of the congregation. Many others, however, do not know the name of the relevant congregation. On the basis that the researcher knows the district in which their ancestors lived (if not, see above for some suggestions on how to discover this), there are several ways to determine the likely or at least potential congregation to which their forebears were affiliated.

For instance, the *Guide to Church Records* produced by PRONI or the lists of congregational records created by the Presbyterian

Historical Society can be consulted. These list the records of individual churches by civil parish. These are useful up to a point, though since Presbyterian congregations are not limited by civil parish boundaries, researchers should also check the availability of records for neighbouring parishes. Brian Mitchell's volume, *A New Genealogical Atlas of Ireland* (2nd edition, 2002), is also worth consulting for it includes maps showing the distribution of Presbyterian churches in the nine counties of Ulster.

Online Ordnance Survey maps can also be helpful in pinpointing churches. For Northern Ireland, PRONI and Land and Property Services have digitised and made available on the PRONI website (www.nidirect.gov.uk/services/search-proni-historical-maps-viewer) a series of editions of Ordnance Survey maps from the 1830s onwards. These maps, mapped at a scale of 6 inches to the mile, show townland boundaries and identify churches (and generally specify the religious denomination of that place of worship). The GeoHive website has first edition 6-inch Ordnance Survey maps (1837–42) for all of Ireland as well as the 25-inch Ordnance Survey maps for the Republic of Ireland (1888–1913).

Do not assume, however, that your ancestors attended the church nearest to where they lived. For all sorts of reasons people travelled to a more distant place of worship each Sunday. In the case of my own family, my father was baptised in Bready Reformed Presbyterian Church, my grandfather in Magheramason Presbyterian Church and my great-grandfather in Dunnalong Church of Ireland – not just three different churches, but three different religious denominations, all while the family was living on the same farm.

What is a townland?

In Presbyterian records – and in most other Irish genealogical sources – the address given for a particular individual or family will usually be the townland in which they lived. The townland is a land division that is unique to Ireland and the townland system has been in existence for centuries. Across Ireland as a whole there are over 60,000 townlands and they average in size 300–350 acres. The word has its origins in the Old English word 'tun', meaning farmstead or settlement. By the early nineteenth century 'townland' had become a general term for a number of local words for small units of land. The meanings of townland names reflect many different things, including local geography, family names, animals, plants and folklore. It is also important to acknowledge that numerous 'unofficial' place-names are found within townlands. Two important online sources of information on townlands are: the Placenames Database of Ireland (www.logainm.ie/en/) and the Northern Ireland Place-Name Project (www.placenamesni.org).

Find out what is available online

The primary purpose of this book has been to draw attention to the range of Irish Presbyterian records that exist and to identify the archives where these may be found, either in original hardcopy format or on microfilm, or even as photocopies. However, as every family historian knows, over the last two decades and more the Internet has revolutionised genealogy. The websites referenced in this book tend to be those of the major archives and libraries. That is not to deny the value of details hosted elsewhere, but researchers will be well aware that websites come and go and know the frustration of broken links. The single largest online collection of Presbyterian baptisms and marriages can be found on the website of the Irish Family History Foundation (www.rootsireland.ie), though coverage varies considerably. Probably the best way of finding out if the registers of a particular Presbyterian congregation have been digitised and made available online is to use a search engine such as Google. For a broader look at what is available online, see Chris Paton, *Tracing Your Irish Family History on the Internet* (2nd edition, 2019).

Examine all congregational records

If registers of baptisms and marriages are available for the time period in which your ancestor was born or married, then obviously they should be consulted in the first instance. If you are unsure of a date of birth or marriage a broad search of the records is recommended. Searching ten or more years either side of the presumed date of the event can produce positive results. Even if an ancestor was born after the introduction of civil registration of births in 1864 it is worth checking to see if a record of baptism can be found for occasionally these include details that are not recorded on the official birth certificate. For example, the register of Portrush Presbyterian Church includes the baptisms on 26 May 1884 of Anne Jane, Sarah and Mary, triplet daughters of Robert Lamont and his wife Mary Ann Cain, residents of Ballyreagh. The following notes have been added: 'This triplet birth Her Majesty the Queen honored with the Royal Bounty of £3 stg', and 'The first in 42 years!' (MIC1P/415).

If registers of baptisms and marriages are not available for the relevant time period other congregational records should be examined. The range and usefulness of these has been highlighted in Chapter 5. For example, even though relatively few Presbyterian churches have registers of burials prior to the twentieth century, the death of a member may be recorded in the Session book or the congregational accounts may include expenditure relating to funerals (especially if the deceased was counted among the poor of the congregation). Neither should the records of the higher courts of Presbyterianism be disregarded for as revealed in Chapter 6 these can also include information on individual Presbyterians. Likewise the personal papers of a minister (Chapter 7), such as a diary, may contain invaluable information.

Find out if there is a history of the congregation

The value of congregational histories has been emphasised in Chapter 2, where it was demonstrated that often these can contain information not in the public domain or which might otherwise be difficult to access. If you know the name of the congregation to which your ancestors belonged, then checking whether a history of that church exists is recommended.

Consider sources beyond Ireland

While this book is concerned with resources for researching Presbyterian family history in Ireland, it cannot go unsaid that information of relevance can be found in many different archives around the world. For instance, some presbytery records can be found in the National Records of Scotland (see Chapter 5). Chapter 11 highlights some invaluable records concerning Presbyterian congregations in Ireland that are on deposit in archives in Britain. In Chapter 7 attention is drawn to the diary and memorandum book kept by two early eighteenth-century Presbyterian ministers in Ulster, respectively, William Holmes and Archibald Maclaine, which are now in repositories in the United States. The value of transfer certificates, very often issued to people on the eve of emigration, is highlighted in Chapter 5 and many of these are in the possession of the descendants of the families to whom they were granted.

The records of churches beyond this island can include references to the baptism, marriage and disciplining of Irish Presbyterians, as well as practical and financial support offered to those who left Ireland during periods of crisis. For instance, in 1692 James Fulton was accused by the Dumfries Kirk Session in Scotland of having bigamously married a woman in Dumfries despite having a wife and three children in Antrim. The Portpatrick marriage register for 1720–1846 includes many references to individuals or couples from Ireland (a typescript of the Irish entries in this register is in PRONI (T1005/1). For other examples, see Karen Cullen's book, *Famine in Scotland: the 'Ill Years' of the 1690s* (2010), which includes a discussion of the movement of Scots to Ireland in the last decade of the seventeenth century.

There may also be references to persons being received into membership on the basis of testimonials issued in Ireland. For instance, the records of the First Church of Wells, Maine, include an entry from 10 April 1720 that Andrew Symington was received on the recommendation of the Presbytery of Strabane of 25 May 1719, the testimonial having been signed by Nehemiah Donaldson, minister at Derg (Castlederg), County Tyrone. For an exploration of pertinent records in the United States, see Dwight Radford, *American Scots-Irish Research: Strategies and Sources in the Quest for Ulster Scots Origins* (2020).

Bibliography

There is no shortage of published works on Irish Presbyterianism and many of these have already been highlighted in the pages of this book. For example, publications on Presbyterian ministers have been considered in Chapter 7. This Bibliography first of all discusses a number of general works, before providing a listing of congregational histories. The latter is not intended to be exhaustive, but is based primarily on the volumes consulted in preparing this book. A fuller list of congregational histories can be accessed on the website of the Presbyterian Historical Society (members only).

General studies

Two early histories of Presbyterianism in Ireland, written in the second half of the 1600s, were by Rev. Patrick Adair ('True narrative of the rise and progress of the Presbyterian Government in the north of Ireland') and Rev. Andrew Stewart ('Short account of the Church of Christ ...'). Along with introductory essays and copious footnotes, these have been published as *Presbyterian History in Ireland: Two Seventeenth-Century Narratives*, edited by Robert Armstrong, Andrew Holmes, Scott Spurlock and Patrick Walsh, and published by the Ulster Historical Foundation in 2016. Another study of Irish Presbyterianism that remained in manuscript form for over two centuries before being printed is *Sketches of the History of Presbyterianism in Ireland* by Rev. William Campbell. This was written in 1803 and was published by the Presbyterian Historical Society in 2019 with a lengthy introduction by Donald Patton.

In the nineteenth century several men, usually ministers, began to write detailed histories of Irish Presbyterianism. Foremost among them was James Seaton Reid who wrote the magisterial *History of the Presbyterian Church in Ireland*, ed. W. D. Killen (3 vols, 2nd edition, 1867). Others works include Thomas Witherow, *Historical and Literary Memorials of Presbyterianism in Ireland* (2 vols, 1879–80) and W. T. Latimer, *A History of the Irish Presbyterians* (1902). Packed full of detail about the workings of Presbyterianism is J. M. Barkley, *A Short History of the Presbyterian Church in Ireland* (1959). More recently, Finlay Holmes produced two excellent overviews of Presbyterianism: *Our Irish Presbyterian Heritage* (1985) and *The Presbyterian Church in Ireland: A Popular History* (2000). A handsomely-produced volume that provides a good overview of Irish Presbyterianism, along with a paragraph on each congregation as well as a photograph of its meeting house, is *Presbyterians in Ireland: An Illustrated History* by Laurence Kirkpatrick (2006).

The most detailed study of the adherents of Presbyterianism in the north of Ireland in the late seventeenth and early eighteenth centuries is Robert Whan, *The Presbyterians of Ulster, 1680–1730* (2013). Andrew Holmes has written two important books on Irish and Ulster Presbyterianism: *The Shaping of Ulster Presbyterian Belief and Practice, 1770–1840* (2006) and *The Irish Presbyterian Mind: Conservative Theology, Evangelical Experience, and Modern Criticism, 1830–1930* (2018). Ian McBride's volume, *Scripture Politics: Ulster Presbyterians and Irish Radicalism in the Late Eighteenth Century* (1998), provides an analysis of the role of Presbyterians in the period leading up to the 1798 Rebellion. It should be noted that these books take a broad approach to Presbyterianism and include information on the different denominations in existence in this period.

Essential reading for an understanding of the Secession Church is David Stewart's *The Seceders in Ireland: With Annals of Their Congregations* (1950). For a discussion of the Secession congregations which stayed outside of the Union of the Synods in 1840, see Godfrey Brown, *The Last of the Seceders: The Original Secession Church in Ireland, 1841–1956* (2017). There is no recent detailed history of the different strands of the Non-Subscribing Presbyterian Church. An older volume that contains much of value is John Campbell, *A Short History of the Non-Subscribing Presbyterian Church of Ireland* (1914). The son of Rev. Robert Campbell, minister of the Old Presbyterian Church in Templepatrick, Campbell had proposed the union of the non-subscribers and played a prominent role in the discussions that led to the creation of the Non-Subscribing Presbyterian Church. He was one of the most distinguished surgeons of his day, wrote widely on medical subjects, served as MP for Queen's University Belfast, and was knighted in 1925. The background to the formation of the Remonstrant Synod is considered in J. W. Nelson, 'The parting of the ways', *BPHSI*, vol. 34 (2010).

For those who wish to find out more about the history of the Reformed Presbyterian Church there are several publications of interest. A detailed study of the denomination can be found in *The Covenanters in Ireland* (1984) by Rev. Professor Adam Loughridge, a former Hon. Secretary of the Presbyterian Historical Society and an indefatigable chronicler of RP history. A shorter and well-illustrated volume of interest is *Covenanters in Ireland: Introducing the Reformed Presbyterian Church* (2012), which focuses in particular on the seventeenth-century background to the denomination. Much more substantial than either of these is *The Covenanters in Ireland: A History of the Congregations* (2010), which contains a wealth of information on the denomination. Running to more than 450 pages, the book represents the work of many hands, most notably the efforts of Professor Loughridge, and was compiled by Geoffrey Allen. An academic study of Reformed Presbyterians in the 1800s is T. C. Donachie, *Irish Covenanters: Politics and Society in the 19th Century* (2016).

Congregational histories

With the exception of congregational histories for Belfast, the following books are listed alphabetically by the name of the congregation.

T. H. Mullin, *Aghadowey: A Parish and its Linen Industry* (1972)

Joseph Thompson, *First Ahoghill Congregation from 1654* (2008)

R. S. Fisher, *A History of Albany Presbyterian Church, 1838–1988* [1988]

Thomas West, *A Historical Sketch of First Antrim Presbyterian Church* (1902)

M. Majury, *First Antrim Presbyterian Church: Gleanings from over 300 years of Presbyterianism in Antrim* (1934)

George Hughes, *Hewn from the Rock: The Story of First Antrim Presbyterian Church* (1996)

H. L. Henry and W. J. Canning, *A Church for the People: A History of High Street Presbyterian Church, Antrim* (1999)

G. Temple Lundie, *First Armagh Presbyterian Church, 1673–1973* (1973)

Fiona Berry, *Names Carved in Stone: The Stories of Some of Those Individuals Who Once Attended the Mall Presbyterian Church, Armagh Before They Marched Off to the Great War* (2016)

Badoney Presbyterian Church, 1844–1994 (1994)

Leslie McKeague, *Trinity Presbyterian Church Bailieborough: The First 125 Years 1887–2012 (Incorporates the churches of 2nd Bailieborough and Seafin)* (2013)

Leslie McKeague, *First Bailieborough Presbyterian Church (Corglass): 300 Years of Worship, 1714–2014 (Incorporates Glasleck Presbyterian Church, Shercock)* (2014)

Belinda Mahaffy, *A History of Ballindrait Church and its People* (2008)

S. Lyle Orr and Alex Haslett, *Historical Sketch of Ballyalbany Presbyterian Church* (1940)

David Nesbitt, *Full Circle: A Story of Ballybay Presbyterians* (1999)

G. A. J. Farquhar, *Ballycarry Presbyterian Church 1613–2013: Memories Fresh and Old* (2013)

J. W. Nelson, *Ballycarry Old Presbyterian Church. A Brief History of the Present Church Building 1710–2010* (2010)

Ballycopeland *see* Millisle

Wilbert Garvin, *A History of Second Ballyeaston Presbyterian Church: Celebrating 250 Years, 1763–2013* (2013)

Jim Wilson, *His House of the Hill: A History of First Ballyeaston Presbyterian Church 1676–2004* (2005)

David H. A. Wright, *Ballylaggan Reformed Presbyterian Church: Two Hundred and Fifty Years of Covenanter Witness in Bannside, 1763–2013* (2014)

Stanley Sherrard, *Ballylinney Presbyterian Church: A Story of 150 Years* (1985)

Jack Leith, *Root and Branch: Wellington Presbyterian Church, Ballymena, 1828–1978* (1978)

A. H. Dill, J. B. Armour, D. D. Doyle and J. Ramsay, *A Short History of the Presbyterian Churches of Ballymoney* (1898)

S. Alexander Blair, *The Big Meetinghouse: A History of First Presbyterian Church, Ballymoney* (1996)

Second and Third Ballynahinch *see* Edengrove

T. H. Mullin and J. E. Mullin, *The Kirk and Parish of Ballyrashane since the Scottish Settlement* (1957)

John Lockington, *Ballyroney: Its Church and People* (1977)

Derek A. Patton, *Settlers by the Sea, 1626–1989: Ballywalter and its Presbyterians* (1989)

H. G. McGrattan, *To Lovingly Make Known: Ballywillan Presbyterian Church from 1661* (2013)

Julia E. Mullin, *The Kirk of Ballywillan since the Scottish Reformation* (1961)

Thomas Boyd, *Scarva Street Congregation* [Banbridge]*, 1830–1930* (1930)

William Wilson, *1623–1973: 350th Anniversary of First Bangor Presbyterian Church* (1973)

Tom Reid, *Trinity Presbyterian Church, Bangor: The Story of One Hundred Years, 1888–1998* (1989)

Brian Cassells, *"The Light Still Shines": A History of Bellville Presbyterian Church* (2012)

W. D. Bailie, *Benburb Presbyterian Church 1670–1970* (1970)

First, Second Boardmills and Killaney Presbyterian Churches: 'The Church in the Rolling Hills', 250th Anniversary Celebration, 1748–1998 (1998)

William J. Roulston, *Foyle Valley Covenanters: A History of Bready Reformed Presbyterian Church* (2015)

Margaret E. Millar, *Presbyterianism in Buckna, 1756–1992: The History of a People in the Braid* (1992)

Trevor J. I. Gray, *A History of Second Broughshane Presbyterian Church, 1861–1986* (1986)

H. P. Swan, *Buncrana Presbyterian Church, 1861–1961* [1961]

H. Barkley Wallace, *Bushmills Presbyterian Church, 1646–1996* (1996)

BELFAST (alphabetically by author)

Jessie C. Barbour, *The Rock in the Plain: Cregagh Presbyterian Church, 1900–1993* [1993]

J. M. Barkley, *St Enoch's Congregation, 1872–1972* (1972)

Robert J. Brown, *Windsor Presbyterian Church, 1887–1987: A Review of the First 100 Years* (1987)

Nelson Browne, *Knock Presbyterian Church, 1872–1972: The Story of One Hundred Years in the Life of a Congregation* [1972]

Hugh T. Combe, *The Dowry of the Past: The Story of Berry Street Presbyterian Church, Belfast, c.1770–1969* (1969)

Roger Courtney, *Second Congregation Belfast, 1708–2008* (2008)

Paul Darragh, *Townsend Street Presbyterian Church: 150th anniversary. History of the Congregation 1833–1983* (1983); incorporates two earlier histories of the congregation by James McCaw in 1933 and William Johnston in 1880

James Dewar, *A History of Elmwood Church with Biographical Sketches of its Pastors and Founders, 1859–1899* (1900)

A. G. Gordon, *Historic Memorials of the First Presbyterian Church of Belfast* (1887)

J. W. Kernohan, *Rosemary Street Presbyterian Church: A Record of the Last 200 Years* (1923)

Samuel Shannon Millin, *History of the Second Congregation of Protestant Dissenters in Belfast, 1708–1896* (1900)

Tom Moore, *A History of the First Presbyterian Church Belfast, 1644–1983* (1983)

William Robb, *Malone: A History of Malone Presbyterian Church, Belfast, and its Neighbourhood, 1835–1970* (1971)

John Robinson, *Centenary Record of First Presbyterian Church, Ballymacarrett, 1837–1937* (1937)

Ronald Ross, *A Day in Thy Courts: The Story of Newtownbreda Presbyterian Church, 1842–1992* (1992)

R. W. Wilde, *Three Hundred Years of Worship, Work and Witness, 1644–1944* [First Belfast] (1944)

John Williamson, *May Street Presbyterian Church Centenary: A History of the Congregation* (1929)

Cahans *see* Ballybay

Harold R. Allen, *A History of Cairncastle Presbyterian Church 1832–1990* (1990)

R. J. McLean, *The Old Meeting House at Carland: Being a History of Carland Presbyterian Church, 1646–1996* (1996)

Robert H. Bonar, *Nigh on Three and a Half Centuries. A History of Carnmoney Presbyterian Church* (2004)

D. J. McCartney, *Nor Principalities Nor Powers: Or Three Hundred and Seventy Years of Presbyterianism: A History of First Presbyterian Church, Carrickfergus* (1991)

George A. Bowsie, *Carryduff Presbyterian Church, 1841–1983, and Memoirs of the District from Bygone days* [1983]

R. S. K. Neill, *A Short History of First Castlederg Presbyterian Church* (1993)

S. W. Thompson, *A Short History of Second Castlederg Presbyterian Church* (1953)

James Little, *Castlereagh Presbyterian Church, 1650–1950* [addendum by his son, D. J. Little] (1950)

Thomas Kilpatrick, *Claggan Presbyterian Congregation* (1932)

Sarah Jennifer McClelland, *The History of Clare: The People, the Place and the Presbyterians* (2018)

H. B. Murphy, *Three Hundred Years of Presbyterianism in Clogher* (1958)

J. W. Lockington, *A History of Clogherney Presbyterian Church* (2010)

J. W. Fleck, *A History of the Clonaneese Presbyterian Churches, 1728–2010* (2010)

Ivor Smith, *Three Hundred Years and Still Praising: Coagh Presbyterian Church Tercentenary* (2008)

J. E. Mullin, *New Row. The History of New Row Presbyterian Church, Coleraine, 1727–1977* (1976)

R. B. Wylie, *A Century of Congregational History, Covering the Rise and Progress of Terrace Row Presbyterian Church, Coleraine, 1796–1896* (1925)

David Clarke, *Others Have Laboured: Terrace Row Presbyterian Church* [Coleraine], *1796–1996* (1996)

W. Osborne Harper, *A History of Second Presbyterian Church, Comber, 1838–1990* (1992)

W. J. H. McKee, *Aspects of Presbyterianism in Cookstown* (1995)

W. W. Reid, *Crossgar: The Meeting-house and its People* (1987)

William Shaw, *A Short History of the Reformed Presbyterian Congregation, Cullybackey* (1912)

Adam Loughridge, *The Covenanters of Cullybackey 1789–1989* (1989)

Jane Megaw, *The Sun-Dialled Meeting Houses, Cullybackey: A Short History of the Cuningham Memorial Presbyterian Church and its Predecessor* (2004)

John Rutherford, *Cumber Presbyterian Church and Parish* (1939)

J. D. Young, *First Derry Presbyterian Church. A History of the Church, 1642–1992* (1993)

Derryvalley *see* Ballybay

J. D. McCauley, *A Covenant Heritage: Historical Sketch of Dervock Reformed Presbyterian Church 1783–1983* (1983)

Joseph Magill and William Harold McCafferty, *Donacloney Meeting: An Historical Survey* (1950

George Eagleson and Tom Johnston, *First Presbyterian Church, Donaghadee, 1642–1992: A Historical Review* (1992)

John Rutherford, *Donagheady Presbyterian Churches and Parish* (1953)

Donald Alexander, *The Parkgate Presbyterians: People and Kirk over Four Centuries: The First Donegore Story* (2012)

William A. Gawn, *A History of Second Donegore Presbyterian Church* (2008)

Wesley and Anna Millar, *On the Banks of the Douglas Burn* (2010)

[W. J. McAtee] *Downpatrick Presbyterian Church, 1827–1977* [1977]

Mary Stewart, *The History of the First Presbyterian (Non-Subscribing) Church, Downpatrick* (2011)

Graham Mawhinney, *The Meetin' House: The History of Draperstown Presbyterian Congregation* (1982)

Aiken McClelland, *A Short History of First Dromara Presbyterian Church* (1963)

W. G. Glasgow, *The Story of the First Dromara Presbyterian Church, 1713–1913* (1913)

W. D. Patton, *The Church on the Hill: A Short History of First Dromore Presbyterian Church 1660–1981* (1982)

Hugh R. Moore, *The Story of a Place of Worship: A Short History to Celebrate the Sesquincentennial of Banbridge Road Presbyterian Church, Dromore* [1988]

J. B. Wallace, *A History of Drumbo Presbyterian Church 1655–1956* (1956)

C. I. Reid, *The Past Revisited: A History of Drumbo Presbyterian Church* (1991)

David Nesbitt, *The Drumkeen Story: A Story of Aghabog Presbyterians, 1803–2003* (2003)

Graham A. Truesdale, *Planted by a River: A History of Drumlee Presbyterian Church* (2003)

S. Alexander Blair, *The Meetinghouse Near the Cross: A History of Drumreagh Presbyterian Church* (1988)

James Mark, *First Dunboe: An Historical Sketch* (1915)

Alison A. McCaughan, *Heath, Hearth and Heart: The Story of Dunboe and the Meeting House at Articlave* (1988)

Alexander Hanna, *These Three Hundred and Forty Years of Witness. An Historical Outline of Dundonald Presbyterian Congregation, 1645–1985* (1985)

C. W. P. MacArthur, *Dunfanaghy Presbyterian Congregation and its Times* (1978)

Dungannon Presbyterian Church: A Short Memoir to Mark the 250th Year of the Congregation's History (1966)

Julia E. Mullin, *A History of Dunluce Presbyterian Church* (1995)

W. D. Bailie, *Bi-centenary History of Edengrove Presbyterian Church, 1774–1974 (formerly Second and Third Ballynahinch)* (1974)

Trevor Magee, *Planted by a River: Two Hundred Years of Covenanter Witness at Faughan Bridge 1790–1990* (1990)

J. R. White, *The Meeting House at Tullanee. A History of Faughanvale Presbyterian Church* (1994)

Joseph Thompson, *The Story of Finvoy Presbyterian Church* (1990)

Historical Sketch of the Gardenmore Presbyterian Church, Larne, 1769–1894 (1894)

D. J. McNeilly and William Burns, *Into a New Century: Gardenmore Presbyterian Church, Larne 1769–2003* (2003)
Glimpses of the Past 1641–1991 [First Garvagh] (1991)

J. A. Todd, *Garvaghy Presbyterian Church, 1800–1954: An Historical Record* (1954)

H. C. Miller, *The Church on the Stye Brae: Gilnahirk Presbyterian Church 1787–1987* (1987)

Glasleck *see* Bailieborough

W. D. Bailie, *The Story of Glastry Congregation (formerly Ballyhalbert), 1721–1977* (1977)

Jack Johnston, *Glenhoy: The First 200 Years* (1979)

Gilbert A. Cromie, *A History of Granshaw Presbyterian Church 1801–2001* (2004)

S. M. Stephenson, *An Historical Essay on the Parish and Congregation of Grey-Abbey; Compiled in the Year 1827* (1828)

David Irwin, *Tides and Times in the 'port: A Narrative History of the Co. Down Village of Groomsport with Particular Reference to the 150 Years of Groomsport Presbyterian Church* (1993)

Thomas Bruce, *An Outline of the History of Presbyterianism in Holywood* (1909)

J. A. Lamont, *Presbyterianism in Holywood* (1965)

James Robinson (with Heather Walker and Janet Taylor), *Presbyterianism in Ulster 1613–c. 1865: A Regional Study with Particular Reference to Holywood, Co. Down* (2015)

Florence Nicholson and Carole Trimble, *The Temple Meeting House: History of 1st Keady Presbyterian Church, 1702–2002* (2002)

Robert Buchanan, *Kellswater Reformed Presbyterian Church, Co. Antrim: A Short History*, edited by Eull Dunlop (1989)

W. J. Baird, *Two Hundred and Seventy Years of Presbyterianism in Killead, 1625–1895* (1896)

W. D. Weir, and H. Campbell, *Presbyterianism in Killead, 1630–1980* (1980)

David Stewart, *Killinchy Presbyterian Church, 1630–1930, with a History of the Parish* (1930)

C. W. McKinney, *Killinchy: A Brief History of Christianity in the District, with Special Reference to Presbyterianism* (n.d.)

Beatrice Elliott and Jennifer Lundy, *History of Kingsmills Presbyterian Church 1788–1988* (1988)

First Larne Presbyterian Church: A People on the Move (2015): includes an appendix by Eric V. Stewart on the early history of the congregation

Classon Porter, *Congregational Memoirs: Old Presbyterian Congregation of Larne and Kilwaughter* (1929); edited and updated by R. H. McIlrath and J. W. Nelson in 1975.

Norman McAuley, *To God be the Glory: The History of Lecumpher Presbyterian Church 1795–1995* (1995)

A. J. Weir, *Letterkenny Congregations, Ministers, & People: 1615–1960* (1960)

J. S. P. Black, *Speaking Yet: Limavady Presbyterians and Balteagh* (1986)

W. I. Craig, *Presbyterianism in Lisburn from the Seventeenth Century: First Lisburn Presbyterian Church* (1960)

Ivan McAuley, *Loughaghery Presbyterian Church: A Chronological List of Events and Developments in the Life of the Congregation during its First 250 Years* (2000)

Joseph Thompson, *Three Hundred Years in God's Orchard: The Story of Loughgall Presbyterian Church* (2004)

Iris Stewart, *Loughmorne Presbyterian Church, Graveyard and Surrounding District* (1994, reprinted 1996)

A. McN. R. McBride, *Lylehill Presbyterian Church 1741–1941* (1940)

Victor Whyte, *Macosquin Presbyterian Church* (1970)

S. Sidlow McFarland, *Presbyterianism in Maghera: A Social and Congregational History* (1985)

Mary Martin, *Magherally Presbyterian Church, 1656–1982* (1982)

Stephen McCracken, *The Presbyterians of Magilligan Ancestry Guide, 1600–1900* (2019)

H. H. Moore, *Three Hundred Years of Congregational Life: The Story of the First Presbyterian Church, Markethill* (1909)

James M. Reaney, *The Kirk at Markethill: A Short History of First and Second Markethill Presbyterian Church* (1981)

Thomas Dunn, *Maze Presbyterian Church: A Short History* (1949)

Thomas Kilpatrick, *Millisle and Ballycopeland Presbyterian Church. A Short History* (1934)

R. Buick Knox, *The Presbyterian Church in Ireland: Minterburn Congregation, 1657–1957* (1957)

H. S. Irvine, *The Big Meeting: The History of Mourne Presbyterian Church, 1696–1996* (1997)

W. G. Strahan, *First Newry (Sandys Street) Presbyterian Congregation: Its History and Relationships* (1904)

T. B. McFarlane, *Riverside Reformed Presbyterian Congregation, Newry. A Sketch of the History of the Congregation for One Hundred Years, 1845–1945* (1945); reprinted and updated in 1984 by S. L. Reid

First Presbyterian Church, Newtownards: A History of the Congregation (1944)

John Brown, *Second Presbyterian Church Newtownards: A History of the Congregation 1753–1953* (1953)

Trevor McCavery, *A Covenant Community: A History of Newtownards Reformed Presbyterian Church* (1997)

Audrey Hodge, *"A Congregation in the Omey": The Story of First Omagh Presbyterian Church* (1997)

John McCandless and Claire McElhinney, *The People of Trinity Presbyterian Church, Omagh 1754–2004* (2004)

Joseph Thompson, *The Meeting House on the Shining Bann: The Story of First Presbyterian Church Portglenone* (1972)

Samuel Gaston, *Third Portglenone Presbyterian Church: A Short History, 1839–1991* (1992)

John McCleery, *Raloo Non-Subscribing Presbyterian Church: A Short Centennial History* (1938)

A. W. G. Brown, *Ramoan Presbyterian Church: A Short History* (1997)

Randalstown Presbyterian Church (Old Congregation) Tercentenary, 1655–1955 (1955)

Robert Allen, *Three Centuries of Christian Witness, Being the History of First Randalstown Presbyterian Church* (1955)

David Magee, *A Story Worth Telling: Historical Sketch of Rathfriland Reformed Presbyterian Church, 1777–1977* (1977)

R. G. A. Morrison, 'A Household of Faith': A Historical Survey of the First Rathfriland Presbyterian Congregation (1962)

Thomas Kilpatrick, Third Rathfriland Presbyterian Church (1924)

Edward D. Smyth, The House on the Hill: The Redrock Story 1799–1987 (1987)

Ivan and Mark Knox, A Hundred Years of Rossnowlagh Presbyterian Church 1906–2006 and a History of Ballyshannon Congregation since 1674 (2006)

David Stewart, Historical Memoirs of First Saintfield Congregation (Toaghneave), through three centuries, 1658–1958, with notices of the history of the parish, and development of the town of Saintfield (1958)

John Edwin Barr, History of Sandholes Presbyterian Church, including the Arrival of Presbyterianism in East Tyrone (1994)

Seafin see Bailieborough

James Glendinning, On the Meeting House Steps: Two Hundred Years of Presbyterianism in Stewartstown, 1788–1988 (1988)

David Killen, Through All the Days: A Presbyterian Heritage, Strabane, 1659–1994 (1994)

S. M. Stephenson, A Historical Essay on the Parish and Congregation of Templepatrick (1825)

S. E. Adair, Templepatrick 1619–1969: The Story of the Congregation (1969)

R. I. Knight, Tullylish Presbyterian Church, 1670–1970 (1970)

Joseph Nimmons, Newmills Congregation, 1796–1947: Historical Sketch (1948)

William Haire and Craig Maxwell, The Life and Times of Urney Presbyterian Church: 320 Years: 1654–2004 (2005)

R. M. Henderson, Waterside, 1866–1966: A Centenary History of Waterside Presbyterian Church, Londonderry (1967)

ARCHIVES AND LIBRARIES

CAVAN COUNTY LIBRARY SERVICE: JOHNSTON CENTRAL LIBRARY
(Local Studies and Archives)
Farnham Street, Cavan Town, Ireland
www.cavanlibrary.ie

CORK CITY AND COUNTY ARCHIVES
Seamus Murphy Building
32 Great William O'Brien Street
Cork, Ireland
www.corkarchives.ie

LINEN HALL LIBRARY
17 Donegall Square North
Belfast, BT1 5GB, Northern Ireland
www.linenhall.com

LOUTH COUNTY ARCHIVES SERVICE
Old Gaol, Ardee Road
Dundalk, County Louth, Ireland
www.louthcoco.ie/en/services/archives

MELLON CENTRE FOR MIGRATION STUDIES
Ulster-American Folk Park
2 Mellon Road
Omagh, BT78 5QU, Northern Ireland
www.qub.ac.uk/cms

NATIONAL ARCHIVES OF IRELAND
Bishop Street, Dublin 8, Ireland
www.nationalarchives.ie

NATIONAL LIBRARY OF IRELAND
(including the Genealogical Office)
Kildare Street, Dublin 2, Ireland
www.nli.ie

NATIONAL RECORDS OF SCOTLAND
General Register House, 2 Princes Street
Edinburgh, EH1 3YY, Scotland
www.nrscotland.gov.uk

NEWRY AND MOURNE MUSEUM
Bagenal's Castle, Castle Street
Newry, BT34 2BY, Northern Ireland
www.bagenalscastle.com/museum

NORTH OF IRELAND FAMILY HISTORY SOCIETY: RESEARCH CENTRE/ RANDAL GILL LIBRARY
Unit C4, Valley Business Centre
Newtownabbey, BT36 7LS,
Northern Ireland
www.nifhs.org/research-centre

PRESBYTERIAN HISTORICAL SOCIETY OF IRELAND
Assembly Buildings, Fisherwick Place
Belfast, BT1 6DW, Northern Ireland
www.presbyterianhistoryireland.com

PUBLIC RECORD OFFICE OF NORTHERN IRELAND
2 Titanic Boulevard
Belfast, BT3 9HQ, Northern Ireland
www.nidirect.gov.uk/proni

QUEEN'S UNIVERSITY BELFAST: SPECIAL COLLECTIONS
The McClay Library, 10 College Park
Belfast, BT7 1LP, Northern Ireland
https://libguides.qub.ac.uk/special
  collections

REFORMED THEOLOGICAL COLLEGE: HISTORICAL LIBRARY
39 Knockbracken Road
Belfast, BT8 6SE, Northern Ireland
www.rpc.org/theological-college

REGISTRY OF DEEDS
Henrietta Street, Dublin 1, Ireland
www.prai.ie

ROYAL IRISH ACADEMY
19 Dawson Street, Dublin 2, Ireland
www.ria.ie

THE NATIONAL ARCHIVES
Kew, Richmond
Surrey, TW9 4DU, England
www.nationalarchives.gov.uk

TRINITY COLLEGE DUBLIN: MANUSCRIPTS & ARCHIVES RESEARCH LIBRARY
College Green, Dublin 2, Ireland
www.tcd.ie/library/manuscripts

ULSTER HISTORICAL FOUNDATION
Bradley Thallon House, 44D Belfast Road
Kiltonga Estate, Ballyconnell
Newtownards, County Down, BT23 4TJ
Northern Ireland
www.ancestryireland.com

ULSTER MUSEUM
Botanic Gardens
Belfast, BT9 5AB, Northern Ireland
www.nmni.com

UNION THEOLOGICAL COLLEGE: GAMBLE LIBRARY
108 Botanic Avenue
Belfast, BT7 1JT, Northern Ireland
www.union.ac.uk/AboutUnion/
  Gamble-Library.aspx

Index

179